Contents

Acknowledgements

I would like to dedicate **Strong Fathers, Strong Sons, Strong Men** to my son CJ and my daughter Malia as they continue to be my motivation for becoming a better Father and a better Man. I would like to thank GOD for inspiring me to be more and do more. Special thanks to Uche, my Mother, my Father, my brothers and sisters, nieces & nephews, aunts & uncles, cousins, extended family, my father & mother in-law, my church family, my livingstone family, all the men that have shown me what it means to be a man and a father, the single mothers that are holding it down for their sons, and all of you that have supported me and purchased this book.

Introduction

One of the most emotional and stressful event in a man's life is the birth of his children. I was told this only days before my first child was to be born. I did not realize how true this statement was until I found myself standing in the maternity ward waiting for hours for my son to enter into the world. Up until that moment, I had more experience at being a world renowned nuclear atomic genetic physicist than I did at being a father and I knew absolutely nothing about genetics or physics. My lack of experience or knowledge in those particular intellectual disciplines was absolutely fine with me as I had no intentions of ever being responsible for having the fate of mankind secretly stored in a vial somewhere in a vault in the middle of the desert.

As each agonizing hour ticked by and with every intense labor pain that my wife experienced it became abundantly clear that my lack of experience and knowledge as a Father could have a more dire consequence if I didn't learn how to be one and learn how to be one quick. In my mind I only had a few hours to learn everything I needed to know about being a father as my newborn son would be here soon. As the hours turned into minutes I increasingly became more upset because for some strange reason the attending physician refused to give me the "instruction manual" on how to be a father like I had asked him to several times throughout the day. I asked the physician repeatedly "Can I Please have the instruction manual on how to be a Father?" He just looked at me and laughed. I wasn't laughing at all, I was serious. My tone became more terse as my wife's contractions became less than 2 minutes apart. I screamed at the physician "Give me the manual man I don't have all day, my son is about to be born and I need that manual." The physician paused and looked at me with a puzzled look on his face, my wife took a break from her labor pains and looked at me like I was crazy and at that moment I was given the devastating news. Sir, the physician stated, "There is NO manual, there is no instruction book, there is nobody coming to rescue you from what you are about to become." I stood there with a panic look on my face as I took in what he had just told me. Nobody was coming to rescue me from my impending fatherhood and there was NO manual. That moment instantly became the most emotional and stressful moment of my life as my wife screamed "I think the baby is coming!!!" I screamed Noooooo I'm not ready yet; I don't have the freakin manual!!! I just kept saying that over and over. I was crying and sobbing with snot running out of my nose pleading "I don't have the manual, somebody Please give me the manual." My wife looked at me with Great disappointment and it was clear at this point to the nurses that I was having a nervous breakdown. One of the nurses pulled me to the side and offered me a little white pill to calm me down. I took the pill and sat down while all the labor events were continuing to escalate. The little white pill had calmed me down enough to gather my thoughts and then I had a sudden flashback. As I was looking at my wife and watching her go through the event that would forever change both of our lives, I reflected on how this would be the last time it would be just the two of us. I remembered first meeting her while we were in college and to me she was the most beautiful and most attractive creature that had crossed my path that day. I've got to have her, I said to myself, I got to get them digits and I've got to get them now.

When I walked up to her the very first thing I said to her was "You don't know this yet but you are going to be my wife one day and you're going to look back on this moment and what I just said to you and you will smile and remember it for the rest of your life." She just laughed and shrugged me off. Five years later, five years of strategizing, straining, struggling, and separating myself from my selfish ways; I found myself standing beside her at the altar, in front of a church full of people, where her father who was the pastor assured me that I could legally take her home with me and keep her forever if I so desired. He then said "by the powers vested in me I now pronounce you husband and wife and I now give you permission to go forth and make me a lot of grandbabies." Everybody laughed including me. Little did I know what that statement really meant. I remember the day my nervousness about fatherhood became all too real. My wife was acting real ornery and she told me she wasn't feeling well. I politely suggested a simple attitude adjustment and some sleep might be just what she needed. She politely suggested that I go in the closet with a dull butter knife and some duct tape and kill myself twice. When she said that, I knew that something was seriously amiss. My wife never spoke to me that way. She was a sweet, caring, soft spoken woman and I knew for her to suggest that I go kill myself not once but twice that something was definitely out of whack. I took her to the doctor that day and I told the doctor that my wife felt like something was wrong with her and I tried to convince her that it was all in her head. The doctor examined her and quickly concluded that it wasn't in her head, it was in her belly. The doctor let us know that my wife was going to be a Mother and I was going to be a Father. The flashback I was having quickly ended at that moment and I found myself back in the maternity ward continuing to fall to pieces as I was about to be a father and I didn't have that dag blam manual!!! I need that manual I screamed one last time to no avail.

I am happy to say and pleased to announce that I accepted the fact that there was no manual, and over the months and years that followed I got the hang of being a father. With the help, wisdom and experiences of a lot of people fatherhood has turned out to be my greatest blessing. I "enjoyed" it so much that I went through that experience again with the birth of my daughter. The second time around was just as scary and emotional because not only did I have a daughter to father but I had a daughter to protect. As a father you love your children unconditionally and you love them all equally but the way you father a daughter and a son are as different as night and day. Each child comes with their own personality, quirks and nuances and there is a huge difference in fathering a daughter than it is fathering a son.

Fathering my daughter I am more concerned about protecting her and being there for her emotionally and letting her know that she is very important to me. I also let her know that I am there for her no matter what and I'm willing to do my best to give her everything she needs and some of what she wants. Fathering my son I am more concerned about raising him to be a well-adjusted, well balanced, well prepared Man. Of course I would also protect him and be there for him emotionally as well but raising him to be a Man while allowing him to enjoy being a boy was often the intended objective of most of the interactions that we would encounter. Why am I so adamant about raising him to be a Man you might ask yourself? The short

answer to that question is: because that is what he was born and destined to be. He even told me with his own mouth when he was a little boy when I was showing him how to shave using shaving cream in the mirror. He said "daddy when I grow up, I want to be a Man." I said you got it little fellow, daddy will make sure you grow up to be a good Man. With that statement, I have spent the last 17 years trying to stay true to that promise. Have I been perfect in my mission? Absolutely not! Have I tried to do my best to raise my son to be a Man? I would like to think that I have but as I stated before there is NO manual. Most of what I learned about being a Father was based on my own personal experiences with my mother and my father and mimicking how other fathers raised their sons.

This book is my attempt at creating a much needed guide so that other fathers and father figures don't have to panic as much as I did when I first became one and made the vow that I would raise my son to be a good man. 17 years later from that eventful day that inducted me into the eternal fraternity of fatherhood I am surprised that the physicians in the maternity wards still do not give out instruction manuals to fathers. They don't give them to mothers either and I'm convinced that nothing can fully prepare you for the task of raising your son to be a good strong man. This is my "manual" and I hope it helps in some way to take some of the ambivalence out of Fatherhood.

As a father of a son that had recently turned 17 years old, and one that would soon be going off to college, I found myself reflecting on the things that I felt my son would need to know about becoming a legal adult and more importantly what I felt he needed to know about becoming a Man. Although my son grew up with me being actively involved in every aspect of his life since birth, I knew that there were still some things that I as a father had not taught him about what it mean and what it is to be a Man. If my own son who had been exposed to positive male role models his entire life still had a lot to learn about being a man, what about all of the other countless young males that did not have the same privileges and advantages? As I communicated on a more grown up level with my son at age 17 I realized that he needed me just as much then as he did when he was a little boy riding on my shoulders as we played in the park. My son and countless others like him not only needed strong father figures but they needed strong Men. Men that would teach them how to be men and all the things that comes with such a role and responsibility. On my son's 18th birthday I chose to give him a gift that he wouldn't find in a store. I gave him a gift of my knowledge, a gift of my wisdom and the gift of my 40 plus years of experiences as a male and a Man. These gifts came in the form of a book that I began writing for him the year before. The book that you are now reading is based on that original book that he received minus some personal experiences and messages that were for him to read and reflect on only. By reading this book, fathers young and old, males of all ages and single mothers raising their sons will all be able to find something that they will be able to relate to and will be introduced to topics of discussion that a father or a man should talk to their sons about as all of the topics are part of him becoming a man.

Some of the topics you will find in this book that sons and men need to know about are: **How To Get Your Children To Become More Interested In You As A Father, Teaching Your Children What They Are Really Worth, How To Be The Type Of Man That Women Really Want, How To Accomplish A Major Goal In 30 Days, How To Be A Giver And Not A Taker, Truths About Women and Relationships, How To Be A Leader At Any Age and Anywhere, Powerful Videos To Watch That Will Change Your Life,** and much more are just pages away.

Preface

On the morning of August 19, 2014, I got out of bed and went through my daily morning rituals of giving thanks to God for waking me up and allowing me to see another beautiful morning and praying for the guidance that I would need to carry me through the rest of the day. I started making my rounds through the house as I did every morning, slowly and quietly opening bedroom doors to check on my children to make sure that they were safe and sound. When I peeked into their rooms I smiled as the low consistent hibernating snore coming from each of them assured me that they were still alive and kicking.

My morning started out normal oddly enough and nothing in particular was out of the ordinary except for the fact that this was no ordinary day. August 19th, 2014 was the day that my son CJ turned 18 years old, reaching the legal age of adulthood and in the eyes of society he was officially considered a man. As the morning progressed I knew that it was going to be an exciting day and as much as I was looking forward to celebrating this important milestone in my son's life I couldn't seem to shake the feeling of a private sadness building up within me. No longer was my son the little bright eyed inquisitive boy with the red Elmo hat on that I used to carry on my shoulders as we played in the park, but standing in front of me on this particular day was a brown eyed male with a faded haircut, broad shoulders, a thin mustache, 5 foot 9 inches tall, and a deepened voice that reminded me that he was not daddy's and momma's little boy anymore. CJ was now a young man, standing in front of me, silently and anxiously waiting for me to give him "the speech." I had been telling him for years that I would give him the big speech about manhood on his 18th birthday as I had already given him the little speech on his 13th birthday and he thought that speech was deep. I told him that his 18th birthday speech was going to be much deeper and more important because he would be a MAN then.

CJ could hardly wait for the day to come when he could finally hear it. As he stood there waiting for the speech, I shook his hand, gave him a big hug, told him how proud I was of him and that I loved him. Then I slowly walked away from him with my hands covering my face as I walked upstairs to my bedroom. I closed the bedroom door behind me, sat down on the side of the bed and instantly tears began to roll down my face like a mini water fall. I sat

10

there for a few moments as I gained my composure and tried to mentally process what had just happened. Deep inside I knew exactly what had just happened. I got up and went back down stairs and I told my son that the speech would have to wait for a little while but that I had something that I wanted to give him. I went to the bookshelf and picked up a book and I gave it to him and told him happy birthday. It didn't take him long before he realized that the handmade book that he was holding in his hands was a book that I had written for him. It was a book that I had started writing for him when he turned 17 years old and I planned on giving it to him for his 18th birthday along with "the speech." To be honest, I initially decided to write the book that I gave to CJ because there were several life altering events that were going on around me that caused me to reflect and re-evaluate my life and the goals that I wanted to accomplish before my dashes in life were completed. As a father I had to come face to face with the real possibility that if something were to happen to me that there would be a lot of unspoken conversations that my children and I needed to have that we would not get the opportunity to have. I became acutely aware of the fact that you can be here one minute and gone the next and whatever you left undone would probably stay undone. As a father of a teenage son and daughter I did not want to leave anything to chance so I began putting my thoughts and plans for my children on paper and planning a "daddy continuity plan" just in case of my unexpected expiration and eternal exit. My continuity plan consisted of many things such as instilling in my daughter her worth as a girl and a woman and preparing my son for the grown up world of being not only a man but being the man in the house. Those thoughts permeated my mind as I was about to give CJ "the speech" on his 18th birthday and thus was the source of my face leaking massive quantities of salt water from my tear ducts right before I was to deliver it.

Writing a book to my children was my way of leaving a piece of me behind so that they would have their daddy's thoughts and expressions close to them whether I was still around or not. I've started a book for my daughter as well but you know "daddy's little girl" thinks she is grown and she has an uncontrollable desire to dictate to me what I should and should not put in her book. Needless to say, that book is on hold until God grants me more patience and restraint to deal with a teenage girl that "knows everything." Daddy loves his little girl. I know she will read this at some point and she will definitely have something to say about what I just said. Anyway back to the speech, the speech was going to be a part of CJ's rite of passage that I had planned for him as he was transitioning into adulthood and in particular manhood.

CJ had already started matriculating at a local college the week before and I knew that I would have to turn loose the reigns. He would have to start creating and forging his own path, making his own decisions and facing the real world on his own with all the potential pitfalls that were awaiting him. His mother and I knew that no matter what we did and no matter how hard we tried that we were not going to be able to shield him from the realities of life, we could only try to prepare him for them. Upon that revelation the morning of his 18th birthday became quite interesting. In addition to receiving the very first version of this book that you are reading, my son received the keys to one of my most prized man toys, the keys to a silver 1983 Nissan 280zx turbo coupe classic sports car with the removable glass t-top roof. Upon receiving the news that he would be allowed to drive "Thundercat" as I affectionately called the 280zx, my son swiftly took the keys from my hands and took off running outside to the silver man toy. He smiled and said "Daddy you can keep the speech that you were going to give, I will take the car." Before I could explain to this hormone raging teenage boy that I wasn't giving him "Thundercat" I was merely allowing him the privilege of driving it, he jumped in the car, put it in reverse, backed out of the drive way onto the street and just sat there with the engine revving. Vroom Vroom the engine growled as my "boy" was about to pull off with my "midlife crisis" toy. My son paused and he looked at me, slowly putting on his aviator sunglasses as he revved the engine again. He threw up the deuces sign, turned up the volume on the stereo system and skedaddled into the sunset. As I saw my firstborn and the 280 quickly fading into the horizon I could hear the song "Cats in The Cradle" by Harry Chapin playing in the back of my head. I took a deep breath and walked back up the driveway thinking to myself where did all the time go? As my son was fading into the sunset I heard the deep throaty grunt of Thundercat as CJ was getting on it good. I could only imagine the smile that it put on his face as I had experienced it several times. As the grunt of Thundercat grew faint and I could no longer hear it in the distance I was determined more than ever to make sure that my son would receive the guidance and support that he would need on his journey to Manhood. Not because he was naïve or oblivious to the road that he would have to travel but because that "boy" had grown up to be just like me, the boy was just like me. If you have never heard the song "Cats in The Cradle" by Harry Chapin **pause right now,** put the book down and play the song on your phone or listen to it on YouTube then come back and pick up where you left off. **Do it now. Don't read another line until you do.**

The song Cats In The Cradle was featured in a Nissan commercial during the Super Bowl in February of 2015. When I saw that commercial I thought about my son driving away in that Nissan 280zx on his birthday and that song hit so close to home for me to the point that I had to get up and leave the room before my face started leaking salt water again. For those of you that did not pause and listen to the song, it's a song about a father and his son and how his father was so busy making a living and doing other things that he never got the chance to spend quality time with his son and his son basically grew up without him. By the time the father realized this, his son was grown and had moved on with his life. If you have a son or know a young man that needs the guidance of a Man in his life please find him some positive male role models that can help you to guide him into Manhood. Good male role models can be found everywhere. You can go visit a reputable local graduate fraternity chapter and express your desire for good male role models. You will find plenty of them there that would be honored to help you guide your son on the right path. Find a local male mentoring program that has a track record of successfully mentoring young males or you can go to your local house of worship and express your desire for a mentor for your son or male youth. Having strong positive honest Fathers, Men and male role models in your son's life is crucial now more than ever and **Strong Fathers, Strong Sons, Strong Men** is a resource that can help you in pointing a young male in the right direction and will aid in his transition from becoming a male to becoming a Man. This book is written in a conversational manner that speaks to the fathers, sons and men simultaneously. As you are reading this book and if you get a sense that I'm speaking directly to you then take that as a sign that something was said that you as a man really needed to hear either for the first time or as a reminder.

Chapter 1

"The Importance Of Strong Fatherhood"

When a child's father is absent from the home or when that child's father is present in the home there is no denying that there is a significant difference in the developmental and behavioral issues of that child. In this chapter we will take a crucial look into the important role that fathers must play in the lives of their children. I don't believe in beating around the bush so we are going to jump right into this conversation. The first area of discussion we must address is what key attributes and characteristics makes for a good strong father and father figure? I overheard a young lady talking to one of her friends on the phone the other day and I overheard her say; "Clavon is a good father to little Nuck Nuck, he babysits him twice a week while I'm at work." I'm going to pause right here for a minute and let what she just said sink in. Yes you heard her right, her baby daddy Clavon is a "good father" because he babysits his son little Nuck Nuck twice a week while she goes to work. I just heard a whole city of women scream bull dung!! I'm going to pause again to make this public service announcement to the men; You should NEVER be caught "babysitting" your own child. I don't think I need to say anything more on that subject. There is a huge difference between fathering a child and being a father to a child.

In fairness to the fathers that were probably raised in a home without a father figure and has never been taught what a good father looks like let's take a look at a few distinct attributes that one should have.

Characteristics of a Good Father

Bread-winner- A good father should be a bread-winner. In this world nothing in life is free and if you are going to acquire even the basic necessities of life such as food, shelter or clothing there is going to have to be some type of currency exchanging hands. What type of currency that may be is totally up to the person that is in possession of that which you desire or need. In most cases the desired exchange currency is money. As a father it is your duty to have some form of currency that will be able to be exchanged for the basic necessities that your child needs. It doesn't really matter how much you have but what does matter is that you have enough to be able to take care of your offspring and provide them with a reasonably safe and comfortable environment.

Nurturing- a father should always be encouraging his children to develop and grow into the best persons that they can become. There is nothing more motivating and encouraging to a child than having the support, security and belief of a strong father that makes them feel like they can do and accomplish anything.

Involvement- interactive involvement in every aspect of your child's life gives your child an amazing gift which is you. There is nothing that you can give your child more valuable or more important than your time and attention. Giving this to your child as often as possible is like writing them a blank check to a life of feeling happy, important and accepted and this will lead to a more well balanced and well-adjusted child and later on an adult

Sense of Stability- being a stable and secure father gives your children the comfort level and confidence to be themselves and to enjoy a childhood free from instability and insecurities. Your emotional, mental, physical and fiscal stability as a father will help to solidify your position as a leader and respected father figure in the life of your child. There is a big difference between change and instability.

Spiritually and Morally Mature-As a father you should be the example to your children as to the moral code that your family unit should be living by. While there may be times that you do not always practice what you preach you should always be aware of the potential consequences that may fall upon you and your family when you are not committed to a life of high moral character. You as a father should be in tune with the spirit that permeates your home and the environment that your children are in. Always strive to live a life of spiritual discernment, spiritual awareness and spiritual connectivity that bring harmony, balance and peace to your life.

There is no one set standard of what a strong father should look like as fathers are as varied as they are diverse. The term Strong Father as used throughout this book encompasses the idea that a father should be mentally, emotionally, physically and spiritually strong enough to carry out his role effectively as a father.

The key motivating factor in me writing this book is the disturbing epidemic in our communities and in our country which is the epidemic of the alarming number of children growing up without fathers or father figures in their homes and a lot of these children do not have a father or father figure in their life at all. It has become such a norm in all segments of our society that some has referred to this current state of affairs as the "Fatherless America". The absence of fathers in the lives of our children is a critical problem. It is estimated that more than 27 million children which is approximately 39% of all US children now live apart from their fathers. An even sadder statistic is the fact that in a typical year, well over one-third of these children won't even see their dad this year at all. More than half of all European-American children and three-quarters of all African-American children born since 1975 will live some portion of their formative years with only one parent; and in the vast majority of these cases, it is the father who is absent, missing or disconnected with his family. The costs that are being paid due to the absence of fathers in the lives of their children is extremely high: major increase in high school dropout rates, substance abuse, teen pregnancy, crime and violence. The absence of Fathers also contribute to all types of social and behavioral issues with their children such as anxiety attacks, emotional absence, decreased academic achievement, aggression and anger.

Fathers, by now you should be able to see a huge glimpse of why your role as an active father is so important in the developmental stages of your child's life. We will now take a look at the characteristics of not only a good father but the characteristics of an effective father. While each unique father will parent in his own style and way, there are some characteristics that "effective" fathers have in common. I will not go into each one of these characteristics in detail here as they will be addressed throughout various chapters in the book but they are:

Involvement, Love, Support, Discipline, Time, Consistency, Morality, and Masculinity

It is clear that when a father is missing in the home or missing from a home, the home is at risk for life-changing, life-altering, life-shattering experiences that impact a child throughout their entire childhood and their entire lifetime. What is even more tragic is that these cycles repeat themselves when these children grow into adults and have children of their own. It is a belief that history repeats itself and it will keep on repeating it until we learn from it. On a more positive note there is overwhelming evidence that when a Christian father attends worship service or a house of worship on a regular basis, the rest of the family tends to follow. A study conducted by the American family institute in 2010 found that when both fathers and mothers attended church regularly, about 41% of the children would attend church regularly when they became adults. Surprisingly, when the father attends church on an irregular basis approximately 60% of the children reaching adulthood will be follow suit with irregular attendance as well or stop going to a worship service all together. When the father chooses to rarely attend church, only 2% of children that grow into adulthood will attend church with almost none of them ever becoming a Christian. When this same equation is conducted with the mother, the numbers are not nearly as drastic or dramatic. The foregone conclusion is that fathers have the greatest influence on their children's lives and have the most impact on their becoming a Christian and attending church regularly as adults. These sobering statistics will have dire consequences on the life of your children as I am of the opinion that having a strong spiritual base and level of faith will prove to serve your children well when nothing else will.

This study shows that when the father takes the church, his faith and his spiritual beliefs seriously, almost all of his children will do the same. When your actions as a father sends the message that you don't care about Christianity, the Bible, or the church, then the overwhelming majority of your children won't either. This shows you the critical importance of being a godly father. This also shows you the importance of being a spiritual role model and being the spiritual head of the family. Your position as a father is likened to that of the high priest in the Old Testament. As the priest commits to live and perform his duties seriously and without hypocrisy or duplicity, so too will his family. You must practice what you preach as a father and a man as you cannot fool children. A superb example of this in the bible is when Aaron's son's brought a "strange fire" before the Lord in the temple and did not take the performance of the priests seriously (Lev 10). Aaron's sons Nadab and Abihu were struck dead and the worship of the entire nation was negatively impacted. Your role as an involved and active father is crucial and if not taken seriously, irrevocable damage can be done to the relationship between you and your children. We have seen the following scenario too many times: A man has a child and then leaves that child only to become an uninvolved and absent father. Then, after some time, he has a change of heart and wants to leave his absent fatherhood status behind. In the meantime, the child and the mother has adjusted to their life without him and bringing a formerly absent father back into the home may not seem to be worth the trouble as the scars he left are still too fresh and real. Upon hearing this, the estranged father gets mad or discouraged with the current situation and stops trying to be involved at all in their child's life. This scenario consequently robs the child of a potentially strengthening and beneficial relationship with his or her father, and makes it hard for him or her to have a positive father role model.

While it would certainly have been best generally for the father to have been involved from the start, it is important to find a way when a father is motivated to be better to let him be more involved in a positive way. This is one of the initiatives that I hope this book will spark and start. The initiative of locating, counseling, reconnecting fathers with their children and building healthy, happy, productive, safe, loving, trusting and mutually beneficial relationships between a father and his children. For every child you see there is a father or was a father in the picture at some point. His absence can be attributed to many things but reuniting potentially good fathers with their children benefits everyone.

Following are some guidelines that an absentee or estranged father should follow when he wants to reconnect with and or become a positive part of his child's life after a long absence.

Get stable and show it. *When discuss stability earlier in this chapter and the lack of personal stability was probably a driving force behind a father abandoning his family in the first place. It could have been the fear of responsibility, lack of maturity, lack of money or just not being ready for a family. Whatever the case, may be, the lack of stability must be resolved before a father can be a seriously positive influence in his child's life. So, find local resources to get some training or education, get a job and stay there, and have a place to live that is conducive for a child. Make sure that you are current on the responsibilities that you do have including child support, so that your involvement is more welcome by your child's mother.*

Communicate with your child's mother. *Having to reconnect with your child's mother can be tough for some fathers, but she is the gateway to the child. Express your desires openly and let her know how you have worked on your stability and personal responsibility. Be willing to apologize sincerely, and let her know how much you want to be a good influence in your child's life.*

Learn about your child. *Since you may have been an absent father and uninvolved in your child's life for a long time, you will have a lot of learning to do about your child. Even as a father, you are coming back as a stranger. Be patient and learn all about your child. Learn about what to expect of a child that is your child's age and what they might be interested in. Get on her level and find out about her life - school, friends, pets, hobbies, favorite foods, favorite toys, etc. Putting your child first in the relationship and making it about her and not about you is an important step forward*

Meet in a safe environment. *It is wise to remember that since you are coming from a "stranger position," you need to make sure that you meet in a safe place. That can be at your child's home, at a grandparent's home, at a park or other public place. There will be lots of suspicion about your motives, and it will be important to keep the child and her mother feeling safe and comfortable.*

Learn your child's love language. *Every child has a personal love language - one that best communicates love and acceptance to them. Find out which love language works best for your child and then use it.*

Don't just be a "Disneyland Dad". *You probably have seen the Disneyland Dads - the ones who just want to have fun, take the kids to places their mom can't afford to go, and spoil them rotten, only to send them home to a mom who has to make life run in the daily grind. Have fun with your child, but mix in some elements of real life and stability as well. It may be tempting to make your time together extremely fun, but don't let it become competitive with their mother. You are both essential to your child's life.*

Get on your child's level. *Children can be intimidated by big men that they don't know very well. Get down at your child's eye level when communicating with them. Use words that they will understand - not too big and not too harsh. Respect your child and just be with him or her, at his or her level.*

Don't try to change your child's world. *However their world is, it is there's. Children feel comfortable with what they know. So, don't take them too far out of their comfort zone. If they have certain habits and rituals that they like don't try to change them. Just go with the flow and get comfortable together first before confronting issues that you might want to change.*

Be consistent and predictable. *Children need consistency and stability, so it is important for a father to be that for his child. No big surprises like bringing a new girlfriend into the relationship too soon or changing plans at the last minute. Be where you say you plan to be when you plan to be there.*

Keep your promises. *Relationships of trust are built by making and keeping promises. Don't make a promise you can't keep, and stay true to the ones you do make. If you promise a trip to the zoo next weekend, don't let anything get into the way of keeping it. The more honest you are and the more you make and keep realistic promises, the more rapidly your relationship will develop. Children need fathers in their lives, and fathers need to be responsible for and to their children. These simple* guidelines *will help create the new relationship that both a child and absent father need in their lives and when followed will help improve the odds of making a hard situation better for fathers, mothers and children.*

Chapter 2

"How Much Is Your Son Worth"

The first and the most powerful thing that every father must teach his children is that they are truly valuable and yes their lives matter. These are not just words that sound good as a slogan, look good printed on a tee shirt or the battle cry in protest because a young male's life has come to a tragic end. Your son must be taught that his life matters and that he is valuable first and foremost because of who created him and why he was created. I used to love watching a program on television called the Antique Road show. On this program people would bring in things that they thought were valuable but they wanted to know for sure what it's true value was.

Some of the things that they would bring in looked like leftover trinkets from a bad yard sale that nobody wanted and they would sometimes find out that that trinket was worth far more than they realized. Some of the things they bought in looked very expensive, rare and exquisite and they would often find out that it indeed was rare because it didn't have much value at all. Most of the things that the people thought were valuable were actually counterfeit copies of the real thing. What I learned from watching that show is that before you can assess the true value of a thing you must first know what it is that you have. Knowing what you have and what you're worth is one of the most important and most powerful pieces of information a man can have. Knowing this information is the basis for how your life as a man begins and ends. Pro-life proponents states that life begins at the moment of conception but in reality your life began long before your parents ever even knew each other. Parents are just the vehicles chosen to bring life into this world. I won't go too deep here but just to give you a glimpse of how valuable and how important you are, think about this fact. A painting called

The Apostle Paul by the 17th century artist named Rembrandt sold for $45 million dollars a few years ago. It was an oil painting, a self-portrait of Rembrandt himself posing as what he thought was a good rendition of what he thought the apostle Paul might have looked like. Here's a question, what do you think made the painting so valuable 400 years after it was originally created? Was it the creator or the creation that made it valuable or both? I can all but assure you that the fact that the painting had the name of the creator Rembrandt attached to it and the fact that it was an original is what made it so valuable. Your unique life as a man begins to take shape and assumes the value that is associated with your creator. Therefore, knowing who you are and whose you are is absolutely crucial and critical in becoming aware of your true worth. The sooner you as a father instill this value in your son, the more apt he will be to carry himself as a male or man of value. As a male your son will try to find his value from many different sources but he must always be reminded that he is an original work of art, created in the image of his creator and that he is extremely valuable. Fathers play a huge role in shaping their children in their early years and giving them a sense of worth and value until they are mature enough to realize it for themselves.

As a father, I make it a point to tell my children how valuable they are, not only to their mother and I but how valuable they are to the creator and to those that they will come in contact with. As fathers or parents of young males, it is extremely important that you teach your sons a strong sense of value and his true worth as he will come face to face with a world and society that tells him every day that he is basically worthless. The best way to start teaching your son his value and self-worth is to make him feel valuable, needed and wanted regardless of the circumstances in which he got here. If he can't get a sense of value, appreciation, love and worth from his parents that help to create him, he surely will not get it out in a cold and cruel world that constantly shows him that it pretty much hates him. As a father you must keep in mind a young male's self-worth will more than likely start to deteriorate the moment he receives his first ridicule, insult or bullied for whatever reason. Once you add on the inevitable rejections that he will start receiving from girls and females, by the time he is 17 years old he has the potential to develop a low internal sense of self value and he will be more susceptible to anything that he feels gives him a sense of worth and respect. Unfortunately the things that tend to gives him a sense of value at this point are also the very things that devalue him as a man. Sexual promiscuity, gang affiliation, false swagger gained by devaluing others, valuing money with no regard to how he gets it, smoking, drinking and drugging just to fit in with the "it" crowd. The sad part about all of this nefarious activity is that it actually causes some young males to feel more valued, respected and it gives them a new found sense of bravado and vitality. This is dangerous for a young male because the better this negative activity makes him feel and the more tangible the rewards, the more enticed he can become to falling deeper into this delusional trap. Studies have found that between the ages of 14-18 this is a crucial stage in the development of a young male's character and values. If he has not had enough positive influences, interactions and experiences at this stage of his life to offset all of the negative devaluing experiences that he may have encountered, then it is only a matter of time before he starts to view the negative behaviors that he will start to exhibit as a badge of honor that he has earned. He will start to feel that his behavior gives him "street cred" and acceptance. This is why it is extremely important that young males have strong Fathers, good male role models and Men in their lives that have been through those stages of life and have navigated through that path successfully and have the scars to prove it.

As fathers and men we know the pitfalls of falling for that false value lifestyle and the graveyard, prisons, child support offices, rehab centers, streets and drug houses are full of our young sons and men that fell victims to it. Our sons must be taught and have it instilled in them at an early age that Yes your life matters and Yes you are valuable but the young males must also be taught that they have the choice to raise or lower their value at any given moment by their decisions, behavior and the values that they have within. No one can truly determine your value as a man for you but you. Teaching young males how to value themselves as Men can only be applied in a practical and meaningful manner once young males first know what a Man is.

The first step in this teaching is defining what a Man is. There are several definitions of what a man is and depending on who you are speaking to it can mean different things to different people. A "man" is generally defined by gender, age and maturity level of a male. While this is a pretty good indicator, this does not guarantee that what you see standing before you is indeed a man.

The best definition I've heard of what being a man is can be summed up as follows:

"Being a Man is when your words and your actions line up with what and whom you say you are; then walking in that truth and understanding and accepting your role and purpose in life."

Have you ever found yourself passionately expressing the following phrase: "I'm a grown Man?" If so you probably found yourself saying this while engaged in a temperature rising conversation with someone that wasn't quite convinced of your proclamation. It is often said that if you have to tell someone who or what you are then you probably have not done a good enough job at being that which you proclaim to be.

What is a Man? Simply put: when a male reaches a certain level of maturity and his words and actions line up with what and whom he say he is; then having the courage to walk in that truth and understand and accept his natural role and purpose in life. One of the biggest problems we have in our society today is the fact that a lot of males don't value themselves as men. If today's fathers and males knew their value in relation to the part that they were originally designed to play in the creation, guardianship and perpetuation of life; then I would assume that most men would be walking around like we were the most valuable asset on earth. Since I've worked at an investment firm for a number of years let's take a real world look at what you would be worth as a man if you were a stock being bought, sold or traded on the New York Stock Exchange.

Two of the most expensive stocks you could buy in 2012 was Apple stock which was at a high of $700 a share and Berkshire Hathaway which was at a high of over $200, 000 a share and it is the most expensive and exclusive stock in the world. Now in comparison to those stock prices how much do you think you're worth as a man? To give you an indication of what you might be worth just from a biological standpoint as a man, ask yourself this question, what is the highest child support settlement you've ever heard of $3,000 a month, $30,000 a month, $100,000 a month? Now add up all the additional costs associated with sharing your seed and the cost associated with marriage and divorce then add in alimony which can reach an unlimited dollar amount depending on your financial status. As you can see, your "value" has suddenly skyrocketed well beyond that of some of the most expensive stocks on the stock market. This staggering and sobering thought should always be in the near reaches of your mind as a male every time you put yourself in a position to give your value away.

While this value comparison may sound ridiculous to some of you it is a financial reality for thousands if not millions of fathers who underestimated their value. If you seriously wish to determine your true value as a man, this comparison is a good place to start. Keep in mind that this comparison is not inclusive of all the other tangible and intangible assets of value you possess and bring to the table. It is often stated that women are the givers of life. While this statement sounds true on the surface it is not entirely true. Women bring forth life, but the man is the actual giver of life in the form of his seed. An important part of valuing yourself as a man is knowing the importance and value of your seed. A man can give a woman two types of seeds, his *biological seed* which is able to produce perpetual life and the *seed of his knowledge* which can produce everything else be it physical, material, emotional, mental or spiritual. These two types of seeds are extremely valuable and essential to the fulfillment and completion of a woman and the circle of life in general.

Valuing Yourself as a Man and teaching your sons this is extremely important because the area in which most of us men are quick to give up our value is during the desire and pursuit of the opposite sex. We as men tend to put an extreme amount of value in the intimate act of being with a woman, but very little value in holding ourselves to the high standards that are indicative to what we are really worth. When we value the intimate acts of being with a woman more than we value ourselves and our seed, then we create the illusion that we are getting something more valuable than what we are worth. In reality and in a lot of cases what we are really getting is a few minutes of pleasure, entertainment and memories. When a woman commits this same act with us, she has the possibility of getting much more than entertainment, she has the possibility of getting your valuable seed and we saw how much your seed is possibly worth earlier in this chapter. A woman can live off of a man's seed for the rest of her life if she chooses the *right* man.

25

In contrast, if a man chooses to give his seed away to the *wrong* woman he stands a great chance of giving away a significant portion of his tangible and intangible value and resources. As we get older our value as a man generally increases due to our socioeconomic status, knowledge, wisdom and our ability to successfully understand and live out our purpose as a man. It is extremely important that you continue to build value in yourself and refuse to do anything that will minimize your value as a man. Men do not become men because it's convenient, because in most cases it's not, but men *chooses* to become men because of individual principles, knowledge of self and a clear understanding of who we are designed and purposed to be.

Some would have you to believe that fathers and men are disposable and not a necessary part of our modern day society, however nothing could be further from the truth. You can look around just about any corner of the world and you can see the aftermath of what happens when fathers and men do not value themselves and do not live up to their roles and purpose in life. I realized the value of fathers a long time ago as I grew up watching the fathers in the community take care of their families, raised them up with a moral code and provided for them. Even the fathers that were not in the home, had afflictions and addictions were still able to garner a certain level of respect and value as a father and in the community regardless of their shortcomings. Value and Respect as a father and a man goes hand in hand and if you wish to increase either one in your life then applying the tips that follow are vitally important and necessary. Take the time to sit down with your son and discuss the following nuggets of wisdom.

Ways To Increase Your Value As A Man

Knowledge – *Knowledge, skills, and experiences are "assets" that you acquire throughout your lifetime. They are as valuable to you as money in the bank. I learned the value of knowledge and what it's worth weeks before I graduated college. There were several of my classmates that had multiple job offers waiting for them even before they walked across the stage to get their degrees simply because they obtained prior knowledge of the companies that were hiring recent college graduates. I learned to be an avid reader and I made it a habit to start reading the entire local newspaper every day. I found that the newspaper had a wealth of information in between its pages that would aid me in becoming a well-rounded and well informed person. Information understood is knowledge and knowledge applied is power. I started reading the wall street journal and different business magazines and it wasn't long before I found myself flying around the country in business suits, on jet planes with company officials, with my own corporate credit card and expense account. By educating myself through reading newspapers in addition to my formal education I was able to speak the business language that opened up several doors for me even though I did not have the normally required business expertise. I learned that Knowledge was my calling card to success in whatever area of life I found myself in. As a man you should be reading something new every day that will help you to not only become more knowledgeable but read so that you can improve your reading and comprehension skills. Educate yourself by any means necessary, take classes that will teach you applicable skills that will earn you a living. Learn to master subjects that interest you the most. The internet is a goldmine of information. Google and YouTube have enough information that will allow you to obtain a wealth of knowledge in a short amount of time. You can attend top notch classes, seminars, lectures and training on various subjects from some of the top universities in the country without ever leaving your home. There is plethora of free online courses. I've taken classes and listened to career changing lectures from noted professors from Harvard, Yale, Duke and Princeton and it didn't cost me a dime. I was able to view and learn from these classes on YouTube for free without paying the thousands of dollars that those in attendance had to pay. Knowledge is powerful and can change not only your life but those around you as well. If you earn more money based on your knowledge, you are more likely to spend more money supporting local businesses and causes in your neighborhood and elsewhere. If you are better informed and involved, you can help make sure that wise decisions are made that will improve the quality of life for you, your family and the community as a whole. Knowledge leads to understanding and understanding leads to wisdom and wisdom leads to having something very valuable that you can share with others.*

Become A Problem Solver –*My father is the epitome of how valuable a problem solver can be to his family, his community and to himself. My father is what some would call the jack of all trades. No matter what it is, if it's broke he can fix it or have the resources to replace it. From solving electrical issues to fixing automobiles or building storage houses my father has the knowledge and skills to do it all. If it wasn't for my father's problem solving skills it's quite possible that I may not have become the man I am today because I did not possess the skills that it would have taken for me to navigate through all of the different problems that I had to overcome to be able to take advantage of some of the opportunities that were afforded me. From staying up all night long in the winter cold fixing a blown head gasket on my car so that I would have transportation to get back and forth to work, to putting a water pump in a well so that we could have running water, my father was and still is the ultimate problem solver. Life is full of problems; if you can fix just a few of them you will prove to be extremely valuable to everyone around you.*

Live A Life Of Personal Accountability – *"If you're man enough to do a thing, then be man enough to accept the consequences that go along with it." Those were the words that I spoke to my son when he was 13 years old. These words were spoken to him after he decided that he was not going to wash the dishes like he was told to do. I didn't give my son any options that day because he needed to learn a very valuable lesson. The lesson he learned that day was that there are consequences when you decide to let your mouth and actions write a check that you can't cash. Let's just say that the dishes got washed immediately thereafter and any thoughts he had of pulling that stunt again were quickly rebuked by the recognition of the "after effects" that was emanating from his defiant body. Living a life of accountability means that you fully realize that everything that you do or don't do, everything that you say or don't say and the mindset that you take into every situation has the potential to either enhance or erode that particular interaction; therefore; it is up to you to choose how you want to impact any given situation. The lesson comes in owning that revelation and accepting the consequences or rewards that come with it. I will never forget when I was in college and out of boredom I made a really dumb decision. That decision ended up costing me thousands of dollars over the years and I blamed my decision on someone else. The ramifications of me not accepting personal accountability immediately upon making that decision punished me for years. It wasn't until I fully accepted the fact that I got myself into that situation that I was finally able to get myself out of it. Living a life of personal accountability ensures that you are always aware that there are consequences and rewards for the actions and decisions that you make.*

Give Rather Than Take – *The value of a man is not in what he is able to receive, accumulate or take but the value of a man is what he is able to give and leave with others. The one true way to becoming more valuable is to be of value to other people. The best way to be of value to other people is to give to them. Find* *ways to give of your time, your knowledge, your resources and most of all give of yourself. There is the age old adage that says it is better to give than to receive. The older you become the more truthful this statement will become. One of the greatest things you can do in life is to give to others. Giving not only adds value to those that are receiving what you are giving but it adds tremendous value to who you are as a man. Don't make the mistake of only giving to the people or organizations that you feel are in need but be willing and open to giving to anyone or any cause that you feel can benefit from your benevolence or service. The people that are valued the most in life are those that give to their family, their community and society. If you want to become a man of value then you must become more valuable to those around you. The best way to gain value, is to lose yourself in the service of others.*

Carry Yourself Like A Rare Jewel– *When was the last time you were told that you couldn't have something? That only made you want it twice as bad which in turned caused the value for that particular thing to go up. We will go to great lengths to gain possession of those things for which we are told that we can't have as the scarcity of those things create a larger demand thus giving it more value. To better illustrate this, A few years ago I was in California on a business trip and while I was there I was able to go to Beverly Hills. My business associate and I were walking down Rodeo drive when we strolled upon the House of Bijan. The House of Bijan is the most expensive store in the world. You are not allowed to just walk into the Bijan store as it clearly has printed on the window "by appointment only." From kings to presidents, the house of Bijan dresses some of the most powerful men in the world. People were lined up down the block just to walk by and look in the window of the store knowing that they would never be allowed to go in it. The average shopping trip to the House of Bijan is $100 thousand dollars and the client waiting list is 3 months long. Only select clientele are "invited" to shop at the House of Bijan. The owner of the store designed it that way from the very beginning and the exclusivity of that simple requirement has added an unbelievable value to the reputation of the store as well as to the reputation of the clients fortunate enough to be invited to shop there. Can you imagine the value you create in yourself when you apply this same "exclusive" principle to your time, your energy and your life in general? This principle willprove to be one of the most powerful things that you can do to add value to yourself as a man. When you value your time and energy others will as well. It is best to not allow any and everybody into your inner circle as this has the potential to drain you of your value.*

Value Your Name And Reputation By Protecting It At All Cost- *A good name can take a lifetime to build and it can be lost in one momentary lapse in judgment. Do all that you can to protect your name and your reputation at all costs. Sometimes in life* you will find that all you have is your name and your reputation and you can build or rebuild your life on the strength of those two things alone. A good name is not something that you are automatically given, it is something that you must earn and it is valuable. A good name and a good reputation can and will open doors for you. When you possess both they will go out ahead of you and lay most of the groundwork that it takes for you to build credibility and discover new opportunities for yourself. Know that people will try to say, and do things that will tarnish your reputation and your good name due to their insecurities, egos, jealousy and lack of control over your life and mind. Your job is to always carry yourself with respect, know who you are and know which battles you should fight or flee. The best way to protect your name is to keep it clean.

Get passionate about your hobbies- *What you love to do in your spare time say a lot about who you are and what additional skills and talents you possess. By just keeping focused on doing the things that you love to do, you can learn and earn your way to a profitable new stream of income or business venture thus making you a more well-rounded person and more valuable to those around you as you will have more to offer. Your hobbies can open many doors for you and expose you to new people and new opportunities. Hobbies such as photography, painting, drawing, athletics, playing a musical instrument or fishing can put you into position to become not only valuable monetarily but valuable as to the experiences that you can share with others.*

Develop And Maintain A Moral Code Of Conduct And Character- *To be a man or a person of value, you must always carry yourself to a higher standard than what others expect of you. Who you are is far more important than what you are. Who you really are is the person that you are when no one is looking or when no one is around. That is the person that you must discipline to live a life of high moral standards and a high code of conduct. There is no better feeling than being able to look into the mirror and be proud of the person that is staring back at you. There is no better feeling than being able to go to sleep at night without a guilty conscious or regret of how you conducted yourself in any given situation throughout that day. Living a life with positive core values and beliefs will help to ensure that you value yourself more than you value those things that detract from who you wish to be.*

Be Willing To Stand Alone To Maintain Your Integrity And Principles- *Be strong enough not to follow the crowd if the crowd is heading in the wrong direction or down a path that is not aligned with your integrity, principles and standards that you have set for yourself. It is better to walk alone on the road to righteousness than to walk with a crowd down a path to self-destruction. Surround yourself with positive like-minded individuals that are headed in the same direction that you would like to go. Always try to influence your peer group in a positive way and lead them in a positive direction versus you*

30

being influenced in a negative way and being led away from your mission and purpose in life.

Always Know That You Are Made In The Image Of God – *If there is one thing that should absolutely let you know that you are valuable is the fact that you are made in the image of God. You are not only made in the image of God but you can have the spirit of God in you if you choose and you can take that with you wherever you go. Anytime society tries to beat you over the head literally and figuratively and make you feel like that you aren't worth much, you need to reflect on the fact that God made you in his image and after his likeness and he made you with a divine purpose in mind that only you can carry out. This fact alone can make you extremely valuable because the contributions that you were born to give to the world can only be given by you. Hold your head up and never ever let anyone tell you that you are no good, worthless or insignificant. This simply is not true as you are made in the image of God and a supreme and divine ransom has been paid for your life. If you are good enough for God to offer up a sacrifice for then you should never let any man or woman try to convince you that you are anything less than what God created you to be. Your value does not come from people's opinion of you, it starts with the opinions that you have of yourself.*

Learn When To Cut Negative People Out Of Your Life- *There is nothing more devaluing and draining on your psyche and mind than the constant whining and complaining of negative people. If you have people in your life that are always negative and never have anything positive to say about what you are doing or trying to do in life then you need to minimize the time and energy that you give them. There is nothing more toxic to your value as a man or as a human being than being around negative people that are doing nothing or not going anywhere. They will eventually try to make sure that you don't do anything or go anywhere either. People that complain or have something negative coming out of their mouth every time you see them are not the type of people that you should want to be associated with. People that are constantly talking about the flaws and issues of others are the very people whose lives are usually tore up from the floor up, emotionally and spiritually. They generally do not genuinely like the person that is looking back at them in the mirror and to help them deal with this fact they will tend to try to tear other people down. In their twisted minds they think by doing this that it will build themselves up. If you are around these types of people you need to cut them loose now. They are their happiest when they see that you are not succeeding or achieving the goals that you have set for yourself. Your success, determination and drive can be a sobering reminder to them that maybe they could and should be doing more with their life. To test their loyalty and mindset towards you all you have to do is let them know about something positive that you are doing that will improve your life for the better. Just sit back, listen and watch their reactions. It will speak volumes.*

Motivational Videos On Valuing Yourself As A Man

Please Pause at this point in the book and watch as least one video below before you continue.

A War Between Two Worlds TD Jakes-   YouTube

Tariq Nasheed -Value Yourself -   YouTube

Tariq Nasheed - Being A Man VS A Boy-   YouTube

Value Yourself | Motivation- Nickmtz210-   YouTube

Do You Value Yourself- arash dibazar-   YouTube

Demonstrate Higher Value (DHV)-   YouTube

Book Note Page To Write Down Ways You Will Help Your Son To Increase His Value as a Male and a Man.

Chapter 3

"Daddy's Little Girl And The Role You Play"

Most of the conversations and discussions in this book pertaining to the importance of fatherhood mainly revolve around the relationship with our sons: how sons benefit from having a positive male role model, a consistent disciplinarian, and a masculine father figure that will have a positive influence on their career pursuits and success in adulthood. It goes without saying that Fathers equally and in most cases more so affect the lives of their daughters in powerful, profound and life changing ways.

One of the interesting things that I have noticed in raising my daughter and viewing the relationships that other fathers have with their daughters is the affects that fatherhood has on a daughter's academic and future vocational path. I have noticed that girls that have their fathers in their lives tend to have a higher level of academic performance and as a consequence, higher career success and financial well-being. As you might have guessed, daughters whose fathers have been actively engaged in promoting their academic or athletic achievements, encouraging their self-reliance and assertiveness are more likely to graduate from college and to enter the higher paying, more demanding jobs traditionally held by males. This helps explain why girls who have no brothers are overly represented among the world's political leaders: they tend to receive more encouragement from their fathers to be high achievers. Even college and professional female athletes often credit their fathers for helping them to become tenacious, self-disciplined, ambitious, and successful. Interestingly, when female college students were asked what they would do if their fathers disapproved of their career plans, the overwhelming majority said they would not change their plans. But the daughters who communicated the most comfortably and had the closest relationships with their fathers were more willing to reconsider their plans if their fathers disapproved.

Today's fathers also seem to be having a greater impact on their daughters' academic and career choices than fathers in previous generations. For example, according to a study, women who were born in the 1970s are three times more likely than those born at the beginning of the twentieth century to work in the same field as their fathers. It is safe to assume that this is not just due to society's changing gender roles but also to the fact that daughters that have their fathers in their lives tend to receive more mentoring guidance from their fathers.

Another interesting fact when it comes to daughters is the influence a father has when it comes to his daughter's romantic life, who she dates, when she starts having sex, and the quality of her relationships she will have with men. Not surprisingly, a girl who has a secure, supportive, communicative relationship with her father is less likely to get pregnant as a teenager and less likely to become sexually active in her early teens. This, in turn, leads to waiting longer to get married and having children largely because she more than likely has been taught to focus on achieving her educational goals first. Daughters that have active fathers in their lives are most likely to have relationships with men that are emotionally intimate and fulfilling. During the college years, these daughters are more likely than poorly-fathered women to turn to their boyfriends for emotional comfort and support and they are less likely to be "talked into" having sex. As a consequence of having made wiser decisions in regard to sex and dating, these daughters generally have more satisfying, more long-lasting marriages. What is surprising is not that fathers have such an impact on their daughters' relationships with men, but that they generally have *more* impact than mothers do.

Daughters that have their fathers in their life that and that experience better relationships with men are less likely to become clinically depressed or to develop eating disorders. They are also less dissatisfied with their appearance and their body weight. As a consequence of having better emotional and mental health, daughters are more apt to have the kinds of skills and attitudes that lead to more fulfilling relationships with men.

Research suggests, that one way fathers may shape their daughter's mental health and relationships in adulthood is in the way daughters with fathers in their lives deal with stress. For example, young women who did not have good relationships with their fathers had lower than normal cortisol levels. Women with low cortisol levels tend to be overly sensitive and overly reactive when confronted with stress. Low cortisol daughters were more likely than the higher cortisol daughters (who had the better relationships with their dads) to describe their relationships with men in stressful terms of rejection, unpredictability or coercion. Given the benefits a woman gains from communicating well with her father and feeling close to him, their relationship and communication matter a great deal. Yet both sons and daughters generally say they feel closer to their mothers and find it easier to talk to her, especially about anything personal. This is probably due to the widely held belief that children daughters especially, are "supposed" to talk more about personal issues with their mothers than with their fathers.

Daughters tend to withhold more personal information than sons do from their fathers. Compared to sons, daughters are also more uncomfortable arguing with their dads, and take longer to get over these disagreements than when they argue with their moms. Most daughters also wish their fathers had talked with them more about sex and relationships, even though they admit that the conversations would probably have been uncomfortable at first. Considering the benefits of being able to talk comfortably with their fathers, these findings are discouraging. So how can fathers and daughters forge a close, positive relationship? Some research suggests certain turning points or significant events can draw them closer. Both fathers and daughters said in one study that participating in activities together, especially athletic activities, while she was growing up made them closer. Some daughters also mentioned working with their dads or vacationing alone with him. Her leaving for college, getting married, and having children often deepened their relationship and made it less stressful largely because the daughter gained a better understanding of her father's perspective and because he began treating her more like an adult. In summary, fathers have a far-reaching influence on their daughters' lives both negative and positive. Many still seem to believe that daughters should spend the most time and share the most personal information with their mothers, however daughters miss out if they neglect the bond they have with their fathers. While fathers may find it easier to relate to and connect with their sons, they should make the effort to build a close relationship with their daughter too.

10 Things Fathers Should Do With Their Daughters

Talk to her about boys-*Tell her the truth about boys. As a man and a father you can teach her about friendships, relationships, sex and love. You can teach her how to spot a good man and how to know when she is getting the run around. The idea is to make her aware not afraid. As a Man and a Father you know all the games that boys can play on a girls mind so you must school her on this at an early age so that she is not taken advantage of mentally, emotionally and physically. I ask my daughter every other week if she has a boyfriend or some little boy that's checking for her. Of course she always says no. I told her good, keep it that way.*

Always check her room- *You never know what or who could be hiding in your daughter's room. There is no such thing as "complete privacy" under your roof when it comes to your daughter. No locked bedroom doors and randomly check your daughters room without notice. I went into my daughter's room one day and I found a dog that she had "borrowed" from her friend at school. It was a cute little Pomeranian but it had to go back to where it came from. Always check your children's bedroom.*

Talk to her about being happy with her looks- *As a father you plays an important role in the way a daughter feels about herself. Girls of today are killing themselves to try and keep up with the people they see on the TV, in magazines and in movies. It is important that fathers show their daughters that they are beautiful and accepted just as they are.*

Teach her the value of continuous education- *A religious and academic education is one of the most important things you can give your daughter and there is nothing more powerful and attractive than an adult woman with beauty, brains and a spiritual grounding. Reinforce this with your daughter by not only showing interest in her extra-curricular and religious activities, but by showing even greater interest in their personal development and progress.*

Teach her how to be independent-*Teach your daughter how to pay bills and manage personal finance, basic car maintenance, how to cook and do general chores around the house. This will better prepare her for real world responsibilities when she is on her own or in the future when she finds a mate/husband*

Introduce her to new foods and help expand her palette to help her be more cultured-*Food is a great way to introduce new cultures to your daughter without traveling the world. Try to introduce new meals in the home or when you go out as a family. It will open her mind to trying new things and create interest in getting to know the world- and not just the place she grew up.*

Communicate and Listen - *Give her an open forum to talk with you and express her mind. If you see something wrong, don't be afraid to ask about it. Talk to her and find out what is going on in her life. Get to know her friends and make sure she is comfortable conversing with you.*

Teach her how to defend herself physically-*Women are often thought to be the weaker sex. Show your daughter her how to defend herself physically and verbally. Show her scenarios of when to talk her way out of trouble. Show her when to walk or run away. Show her when and how to fight. Karate or Tae Kwon Do should be on her to do list.*

Force her to spend time with the entire family- *Most daughters would rather be with their friends but family time will teach her family values and feel love from both parents. Random getaways will get her out of the house to explore, learn, exercise, and relax and spend quality time with the family. A teenage daughter's life can be very stressful and a nice family getaway may be just what she needs.*

Be the example-*Treat her mother the way you want men to treat her. Daughters will learn a lot about relationships and how she should be treating by observing how you treat and communicate with her Mother. Always show love, respect and admiration to her Mother and when conflict arises use it as an opportunity to show your daughter how a man should handle it.*

Chapter 4

"The Truth About Women and Relationships"

When I first told my son about girls and the birds and the bees years ago he was not fazed by that conversation at all. We revisited that conversation several times years later as my son became older and more aware that there are some things in this world more interesting than playing video games. Don't get me wrong, there is nothing like the sensory experience of playing your favorite video game on a PS4 or Xbox but there are only a few things that are more entertaining, engaging and pleasing than interacting with a female that catches your eye. I haven't figured out what those things are yet but as soon as I find out I will let you know. As my son became more aware of this fact I kept it as real as possible with him about the role that the female gender will play in his mission as a man.

The average boy and man will spend a huge amount of his conscious and unconscious thoughts thinking of ways to endear himself to the female persuasion so that he can possibly one day add her to his list of "entertainment." This is a fact and as fathers and men we must not sugar coat the role girls and women will play in a male and a man's life in all aspects. I have raised my son to have a healthy appreciation for girls and women and to treat them with respect but I also taught him that true respect must also be earned and you do not give away your value and respect trying to gain the favor of a female. Respect is not automatically given; it is earned in most cases. I also taught him that no matter what female you find yourself involved with that you should always set high standards for yourself and live by a moral code of conduct. That set of standards and moral conduct will mean different things to different people but it is still important that we teach our sons that a standard and a code of conduct should be set so that you are very clear about who you are and what you stand for when choosing to get to know a potential female mate or partner. I will go ahead and make this disclaimer: **What you are about to read next is based on my opinion and the conversations that I have had with women and men over the years. The opinions expressed in this chapter in no way represents all women or even how most women think but this chapter is based on real experiences and philosophies that several women and men have confirmed takes place more often than one may wish to believe. Now enjoy the rest of the chapter.** There are two things that boys and men will do just about anything to obtain and acquire and that is **Women** and **Money**.

Those are the two most powerful creations on earth to a man. It doesn't matter to a man which one he gets first, the money or the women as they are both closely linked to your mission as a man. Throughout this book we will be discussing ways in which you can attract and obtain both but in this chapter we will be discussing Women and the powerful role they play in your life and your mission as a man. Before we get into the good stuff about how do you attract women let's first take it to the beginning as I tell you about a show I was watching awhile back. I was watching a show on one of the television networks and the purpose of the show was to try to help fix a man's life. On this particular episode there was a famous hardcore male rapper on the show that needed fixing and the host was determined that she was the right person for the job. Throughout most of the show this hardcore, aggressive, rapper was bold, loud and belligerent to the female host. He continued to rebel against her attempts to get at the root cause of his relationship issues concerning his wife and his kids. In the middle of this rapper's profanity laced tirade, the host of the show said to the hardcore rapper "how is your relationship with your mother?" The rapper paused for a moment as he pondered the question and said "it's alright, nothing to brag about." You could clearly see his whole demeanor change instantly.

The host asked the rapper again to tell her about his relationship with his mother. At that moment the rapper became completely quiet and he started rocking back and forth in his chair and as he rocked back and forth you could see that his eyes had become watery and tears started trickling down the side of his face. He rocked back and forth more frantically as he put his face in his hands and he cried out repeatedly "she never told me she loved me, she never hugged me, she never wanted me." As his soul cried out, this hardcore, menacing, hulk of a man curled up in a fetal position and wept like a baby. For me, watching that scene was difficult because I know what it feels like when you're rejected by someone that you felt should have liked you, it happened to me in the third grade. I will never forget when I got my heart broken in the third grade. Her name was Carmen (*no Carmen not you, a different one*) and she was the cutest girl in my class. I got up the nerve to write Carmen a note and on that note it simply said "do you like me yes or no, check one please." I had some fellow students pass the note up to Carmen and before she even got the note she turned around and looked at me and said NO I don't like you. Whew, let me take a breather for a second, as I reflect on the pain of that rejection that I felt on that day. It wasn't so much the fact that Carmen had rejected me as it was the fact that she didn't even read my note and my classmates were passing it around laughing. The teacher took my little note and asked who wrote it. I said I did and she said no writing notes in class and she put the note in her desk. I raised my hand and I said to the teacher, "Ms. Mcgillycutty could you please give me my note back?" She said why? I said I want you to give me my note back so I can give it to Jessica (*no Jessica not you, a different one*) who was sitting next to Carmen. At that moment Carmen got furious and I learned my very first lesson about rejection and girls that day. Jessica eventually said No as well but Carmen didn't know that and for some reason Carmen was real nice to me the rest of the school year as long as she thought Jessica liked me... hmmm. Now back to the show I was watching. That rapper's soul and spirit was broken as he expressed his anger and heartbreak about the rejection he felt from his mother. For the rapper, having this deep brokenness to resurface unexpectedly on national television to inflict fresh new wounds was more than he was able to bear. The female host of that particular show went over to this rapper and wrapped her arms around him and held him as he rocked back and forth crying in her arms. The host at this point turned the cameras off, held this broken man in her arms and ended the videotaping of the show. Watching that episode of the show it became painfully clear how enormously impactful a boy's relationship with the first woman in his life, which is usually his mother, can be in shaping and influencing his views and behaviors toward women as he grows up to be a man. I was fortunate enough to have a loving, caring and down to earth Mother and as a result I have been able to pass that along. There is a saying that states: "*No matter how big a man becomes, there is no man that is bigger than his Mother*. The first and most powerful connection your son will experience as a male is the relationship he has with his mother. This relationship, and the love, security and the affection it provides or the lack thereof, will forever shape him as a man and every woman that he will come in contact with will be the beneficiary of this relationship in some way or another. Watching the show Fix My life revealed a deep seeded truth. If you want to break a man down and really get to the root cause of the source of a lot of his behaviors and views he has when it comes to women and relationships, draw him into an honest conversation about his mother. As a father keep this in mind.

This chapter is designed to help males and men to overcome past hurts and rejections from women and view them as a necessary part of life. Just think of this, if women never rejected any man that came up to them, we would never have a chance at getting a woman that we liked because she would have already been taken by the first knucklehead that tried to talk to her. This chapter will help you to become the type of man that never gets rejected and you will learn to become the type of man that the women desire, need and want. Whether it's your girlfriend, your wife or a female family member every woman in your life will benefit when you choose to go from being a male to becoming a Man. In the previous chapter we discussed the importance of valuing yourself as a man. The reason that this is so important is because everything comes down to value when interacting with a woman. When you first meet a woman that you're interested in, before that woman considers you as a potential mate she is calculating your perceived value in her head. She is checking out your physical attributes, your body language, the words that are coming out of your mouth, the confidence in the words that are coming out of your mouth, the way you make her feel when you are around, the way you dress, what you have on, your grooming, the environment in which you just met her in and anything that she feels is connected to you in any way that has any value.

While you are standing there she has calculated your perceived value in relation to who and what she thinks she is. If your perceived value isn't equal to or is greater than what she thinks her value is, then you will most likely not be making her potential partner list at that moment. It is important that you don't confuse the words partner and mate with the words hookup and friends with benefits. Those are two different beasts and the "value" calculations for those two totally different scenarios vary greatly. One tends to be generally a little more superficial. When a woman sees a man that catches her eye *everything* breaks down to Value. I remember an old school playa move called "Big Ole Me and Itty bitty you." The playa move worked like this. When you first met a woman you did not meet her at a club or any event that requires that she dress up and look her best as this environment tends to give her a false sense of security, value and status. In that environment it is easy for her to feel that she has more value than you since she will be getting a lot of attention and she is at her best from a superficial sense. As an old school playa you wanted to meet her in her own comfortable environment where she is casually dressed in maybe a pair of jeans and an old tee shirt while out running errands. When you as an old school playa just happen to "randomly" meet her you should make sure that you are dressed extra crispy in some nice gear, expensive nice smelling cologne, have an eye catching subtle piece of jewelry preferable a diamond of some sort, and that your grooming and your car is tight and clean.

The old school playas drove what they called foreign steel with sex appeal. This was referring to a luxury flagship foreign vehicle such as a 7 series BMW or 5 series Mercedes or any type of clean shiny Porsche. The point of this playa move was to visually overload the female's sensory perception and her perceived value calculation that is quickly calculating in her head. Once her calculation is complete, your initial impression on her should be sending the mental message of look at "Big Ole Me and itty bitty you." For the record, the game of big ole me and itty bitty you is very immature, superficial and a turn off to most women however in a lot of those scenarios the female would think that the playa had high value and the playa would end up getting the female even if it was only temporary. When you meet a female and you are dressed good, riding good, smelling good and talking good it sends a subliminal message to her brain that you might be a man about something or a man of means. When the female starts to think that you might be about something then her next question will probably be what value can you bring to her life? Now don't misunderstand this process that women sometimes go through to weed you out as a candidate for her attention and affection. In most cases, it's a natural defense mechanism automatically engrained in a woman's psyche to ensure that she finds a suitable mate to eventually give herself to and reproduce future offspring with. The truth of the matter is, the woman that just went through the value calculation described above doesn't really know anything about you. All she knows is what she has heard and seen and what her instincts have told her. She has not taken into account all of your tangible and intangible value.

In most cases for a woman to respect you as a man, or be attracted to you she must see you as someone more valuable than herself. She must see you as someone that can do more for her than she can do for herself. You must be able to give her something that she is not able to give to herself, the gift of manhood. By giving a female this gift, your value as a man greatly increases. You must become comfortable in your role as a man and be willing to give the women in your life the essence of your gift which is strength, wisdom, knowledge, understanding, confidence, excitement, protection, resourcefulness, truth, honesty, guidance, leadership and adventure.

When you are able to give these things to a woman your value will skyrocket and elevate you to another level that will have women literally hunting you down and chasing you. Once you reach this level you will truly begin to understand the power of being a man. You being a Man, according to the definition explained earlier, is the ultimate security for a woman. She doesn't really care about your money or what you drive or what you can buy her. You could be broke, busted and waiting at a bus stop. What she really wants from you as a man is security. She wants the security in knowing that you are who you say you are and that you are not going to change on her.

Sometimes we as men start out talking good, sounding good and telling a woman everything that she wants to hear. 1 month, 3 months or 6 months down the road we change up on her and she finds out that we aren't who we made her believe we were. The ultimate security for a woman is in her knowing who her man is and knowing that no matter how bad or how good things get, her man is not going to change on her. She finds security in the fact that he is indeed a man. When you as a man deviate or dissipate from who and what you say you are as a man, your woman has the right to despise you and be angry with you and she will most definitely have an attitude towards you. The only time you should deviate from who you say you are as a man is when you are evolving into someone better than who you told her you were. A woman can't *define* you as a man, she can only *agree* with you being a man. A true man is what women really want, need and desire. A man that provides her with a sense of security, a man that gives her guidance and leadership, a man that is resourceful, a man that can mentally, physically, spiritually and emotionally take her places that she's never been before and a man that is confident and comfortable in his own skin.

Simply put, if you become everything that a woman needs then she will give you everything that you want. You will not have to chase women or try to impress them with your perceived value as she will know that your true value is priceless and that you are the prize.

I was looking in my old high school year book one day and I was reading some of the final year end messages that some of my classmates wrote in my year book. One of the messages was from a friend of mine that was an athlete at our school and by all accounts it appeared that he had everything that the girls in high school would want in a guy. The message he wrote in my year book was "Good luck in whatever you choose to do but whatever you do please tell me how to get the women." His message struck me as a joke back then but reading it years later the more I realize that he was asking the question that all of us young boys back then wanted to know and what most of us men are asking ourselves now. How do we get the women?

The next couple of pages you will find valuable tips on how to get and keep the women that you will come in contact with through various stages of your life. I was "fortunate" as a young man coming up because I had some older brothers and male friends that seemed to have a knack for meeting and attracting a lot of different women. These guys were not the most attractive, not the flashiest or the most athletic guys in the world but they had a few things that a lot of guys didn't have and that was confidence, charisma and a natural desire to enjoy life to the fullest. Looking back I don't even think they even knew what it was about them that caused them to attract such a high level of interests from females back then. They probably just thought like most guys thought that could get females, "I am the shiznizzle." (I don't cuss or curse so shiznizzle is the best I can describe the word I really wanted to use.) I slowly learned what confidence and enjoying life could do for a young male's psyche and self-esteem and the part it played in attracting the girls and later the women. I tried to emulate the behavior of my older brothers and friends as best as I could but for some reason it just wasn't working for me like it did for them. As I matured and started to really like who I was and what I thought I had to offer my "game" improved and I unofficially became a protégé of the males that I was learning from. I liked the girls and miraculously the girls started to like me back. I thought I had conquered the game of getting girls because I had finally got them to like me. Little did I know that getting them to like you was only the beginning.

45

What do you do next I asked my older brothers and friends? As a young male still in junior high school at that time, the true answer to that question should have only came from a Father or a Man and not other young males that were still trying to find themselves and really didn't know anything about the real deal when it came to girls and relationships. All they knew is that the "game" they were playing was working. The reality that I was too young to realize is that the reason the game was working back then for them was because it was being played on the minds and the naiveté of other young females that desperately needed a father figure or man in their life as well to school them on the real deal about relationships and the opposite sex. In the defense of the men and father figures that tried to steer their young sons in the right way back then, you know all too well how hardheaded a hormone raging teenage boy can be and the only advice he wants to hear is how to get more girls.

When I think back to the third grade when I was trying to get Carmen and Jessica to like me I realize that instinctively I had what it took to later attract older females. I was bold as I didn't give it a second thought to give both of them the "do you like me" letter. I had confidence in myself and was convinced that they both would say yes. I learned that rejection is a part of life and how you rebounded from it is what was most important. You will find as a young male and as a man that some of the best times of your life will be experienced with a female somewhere in the picture. Whether it's spending time with your mother or grandmother enjoying a good conversation, hanging out with your sister at a forbidden gansta rap concert, going on vacation with just you and your wife, combing your daughter's hair and putting it in a style that she actually likes or just having the support of the women in your life whenever you decide that you want to try another "crazy idea" that you feel will benefit not just you but her as well. Women will play a huge role in your life as a male and as a man. The better you are at interacting with females and understanding them the better your life will be. It is the responsibility of a Man to teach the young males the truth about the role women will play in their lives and how they should respond to that fact. Here is another disclaimer: A male or man can never truly understand the inner workings of a female's mind no matter how much experience you think you have with them.

The tips that follow are not tips of manipulation or some pick up line that you use. These tips are not magical words or phrases that I picked up in a hocus pocus spell book. These tips are about things that will increase your chances of becoming more attractive to females and women and are designed to help you to become the type of man that all types of women and females would like to be around. Use the tips carefully as they can have a profound positive effect on your dating life and in your relationships with women in general. I made the statement earlier that these tips will help you to never be rejected by a woman. The key to that statement is in the fact that when you are busy being a Man you will not have to chase women they will start to chase you. For some young males this section on attracting women is probably a little too deep at the moment for them to really soak in because they probably just want to go Ron Propeil on a chick. Ron Propeil was a guy in a television infomercial where he didn't have time to cook anything, he just threw some stuff in what looked like a toaster oven and he closed the door on it, hit a button and walked off and went and did whatever else he had to do. Ron Propeil would come back to the toaster oven ten minutes later and Waa Laa his entire meal was done, cooked to perfection as he would say. He used the phrase "all you got to do is set it and forget it." As a male there is a phrase similar to this that you may have heard other males use and it's the phrase "hit it and forget it." As a young male this may sound like a quick and easy way to interact with a female but a Man knows that long after you have consumed the meal that was cooked in the toaster oven that the after effects of it will last long past the ten minutes it took for you to cook it. I told my son this analogy and he looked at me like I was some dishes that needed to be washed, with bewilderment and resistance. It is extremely important that fathers teach their sons as much as possible about the role girls and women will play in their son's life. You should make it comfortable for your son to come talk to you about anything and you owe it to him to be as truthful and as honest as you deem necessary. Sometimes, the ugly truth is better than a pretty lie when it comes to teaching your son about relationships and attracting women as women will play a huge role throughout his entire life.

Tips For Single Men That Will Make Women Interested In You

Be Confident – *Do You Like Me Yes or No? That was the question as I rode up to this girl on my bike in the 7th grade. I slid my wheels, kicked up dust, put my kick stand down and looked her dead in the eye and I said "Do you like me yes or no, my brother said you liked me." She looked at me at started laughing as she walked away. Do you like me I shouted? She turned and looked back and said NO. I was shocked, heartbroken and flabbergasted I didn't know what I had done wrong. Was it my huffy bike, the dust, my cloths, did I look good enough? I had felt my second sting of female rejection. I went over to my brother and I said I thought you said she liked me. He started laughing hysterically. He said your brother bet me that you wouldn't go over there and talk to her and I won the bet because you did. I learned a valuable lesson that day that I would not realize until years later. The reality of that encounter was that my brother lied to me and that girl never said she liked me. She didn't even know me. The beauty of that encounter was the fact that it gave me the confidence to go up to a girl that I normally would not have had the heart to even speak to. Because of the belief in my head that she already liked me it changed my whole attitude and I got on my bike and rode up to her with pure confidence and talked to her. I saw that same girl 28 years later at that same spot at a church function. This time I pulled up to her on my Kawasaki ZX1100 sport motorcycle, put my kick stand down, took off my helmet, looked her in the eye and said "Do you like me, my father in law said you like me." She looked at me and said you are so silly, as she and my wife laughed hysterically and walked away. Confidence is king.*

Make Her Feel Comfortable – *You must become comfortable with making a woman feel comfortable around you at all times. The best way to do this is to show her what you would be like as a boyfriend without telling her that's what you are doing. If you want to make a girl feel comfortable around you, you have to treat her like she's already your girlfriend. If you have a woman that is casually interacting with you on the regular, in her subconscious mind she is trying to decide if you would be a good companion for her, whether she consciously realizes this or not. The more comfortable you are with yourself, the more comfortable she will feel being around you, and thus, the more attracted she will be to you. One of the best ways to make a woman feel comfortable around you is to have autonomy. Autonomy simply means that you have the freedom, the will and the privacy to* do whatever you want. You don't have to answer to anyone about the time you spend with her or when she can come over, you have complete control over all of that. To be autonomous you must have your own place, this means that you do not have any roommates or anyone that you have to share your domicile with. You can't be living with your mama. You must have the keys to your own private spot that you can take a female to where she can feel safe and comfortable. It doesn't have to be an expensive or trendy place but it must be very clean and masculine with a small touch of feminine energy. The basic accoutrements that you must have in your spot is a flat screen tv, a nice soft sofa, some of her favorite beverages in the refrigerator, fruit, women's magazines on the table, nice big bed with a headboard, candles, massage oils, lotions, a good sound system and a nice collection of music. Preferably you want to have music with no words because you don't want the music to cause her to start reminiscing about some other dude or event in her life. Smooth jazz or instrumental music usually does the trick .To really make her feel real comfortable with you at this point, just sit back, relax, shut up, listen and enjoy wherever the evening leads you. You should not try to initiate anything in terms of physical intimacy at this point. You're not ready for that yet. That's my public service announcement for the young bloods.

Be The Rare Jewel– When was the last time you were told that you couldn't have something? That only made you want it twice as bad which in turned caused the value for that particular thing to go up. We will go to great lengths to gain possession of things and people for which we are told that we can't have. Because of the scarcity of those things a larger demand is created thus giving it more value. To better illustrate this, I was in California on a business trip and while I was there I was able to go to Beverly Hills. My business associate and I were walking down Rodeo drive when we strolled upon the House of Bijan. The House of Bijan is the most expensive store in the world. You are not allowed to just walk into the Bijan store as it clearly has printed in regal letters on the building "by appointment only." People were lined up down the block just to walk by and look in the window of the store knowing that they would never be allowed to go in it. The average shopping trip to the House of Bijan is $100 thousand dollars and the client waiting list is 3 months long. Only select clientele are "invited" to shop at the House of Bijan. The owner of the store designed it that way from the very beginning and the exclusivity of that simple requirement has added an unbelievable value to the reputation of the store as well as to the reputation of the clients fortunate enough to be invited to shop there. Can you imagine the value you create in yourself when you apply this same "exclusive" principle to your time, your energy and your life in general? This principle will prove to be one of the most powerful things that you can do to add value to yourself as a man. It is almost necessary to use this principle at some level if you plan on attracting and keeping women interested in you. People in general tend to value things that are rare and that are hard to obtain. Women are no different. The more rare or scarce a thing is, the more value it tends to have. By becoming a rare and valuable man your value will skyrocket.

Be Fun, Be Adventurous, Be Unpredictable– *If you are fun to be around, can make a woman laugh and you can give women new adventures that they enjoy, then they will line up in droves to go out with you. I remember the first "date" I went on with my wife. It was a Christmas party while we were in college. I got all dressed up and I walked over to my future wife's dorm and escorted her to the Christmas party. On the way to the party I told her that I was her escort, her bodyguard and her personal entertainment for the evening. From the moment we walked into the door we laughed, talked, danced, ate, people watched and talked about various topics. I pretended to be Santa Claus as she sat on my lap. Afterwards I gave her a walking tour of some of the secret spots on campus that she had never seen and at each spot we stopped at I had a friend of mine waiting there with a gift to give her. She ended up with 5 Christmas gifts that night and none of them cost more than one dollar. I was fun, adventurous, spontaneous and unpredictable and she could never figure me out completely. This will always keep a woman interested in you. Go do something different and adventurous and be unpredictable.*

The Woman Has To Like You- *This goes without saying but if you're going to attract women you have to be the type of man that women like and like being around. Listening to a woman and being the source of peace, comfort and joy goes a long way in becoming the type of man that women find desirable. You will find out that a lot of times having a woman liking you is more important than having a woman loving you. When a woman likes you this is generally driven by the actions and behaviors that you have displayed and how you make her feel at any given moment. When a woman loves you, it's more about how a woman feels about her commitment to the relationship you two share regardless of how you make her feel on any given day. A woman can love you and hate your behavior at the same time. Be Likeable.*

Form Friendships With Attractive Females- *Women are attracted to high value desirable men that can't easily be obtained. Women are even more attracted to a man that has other attractive women that are attracted to him as well. How many people would want something that nobody else wanted? Not too many. The more women that a woman thinks is attracted to you the more your value in her eyes will increase. The higher the value a man has, the higher the attraction will be. Make it a habit to strategically surround yourself with attractive women and genuinely try to become friends with them. This will instantly make you more attractive to women as they see that other attractive women find value in you. If you're at work be seen eating lunch with the most attractive women you can find. Meet beautiful women with the intentions of just becoming a good friend and nothing else. Be seen with beautiful women of all races, sizes and nationalities. This will help you to become use to being around beautiful women and will make you less likely to fall for looks alone when looking for a woman to enter into a romantic relationship with. The beautiful thing about hanging out with beautiful women is that in most cases you will discover that* *their true beauty is actually on the inside of them waiting to be discovered.* I just dropped you a jewel with what I just said fellas. Use it with caution as it can be a dangerous and powerful tool in your quest to attract the ladies.*

Stand Out From The Crowd - *If you want to attract women find a way to separate yourself from being merely average. If you have a unique talent or skill such as playing a musical instrument, an athlete, a dancer, artist or fashion trend setter don't be afraid to let people see that side of you. Standing out from the crowd will not only separate you from the perception of being average but it can enhance your persona of being an independent and interesting man. Having a unique style of dress, an accent or cool hairstyle or wearing a pair of nice shades and staying in good physical condition will get you noticed and help you to stand out. You don't have to "peacock" around to stand out. Just let whatever makes you unique and interesting stand out.*

Intelligence And Articulation - *As a Man, being well spoken and intelligent will allow you to meet and converse with women from all walks of life. Whether you're at the grocery store, in a lounge, at the gym or at a corporate retreat, being and sounding intelligent will make you a very attractive prospect for several different types of women. Increase your intelligence by gaining knowledge on a wide variety of issues, concerns, causes and current events that affects women as a whole. Become an expert on a particular topic or in a certain field. Study and read everything you can find on a particular subject that matters to most people and become an expert on that subject. The words that are coming out of your mouth can be extremely powerful and influential and should be chosen with care. Being able to verbally communicate in a manner that captivates a female's imagination and imparts her with knowledge is a skill that you will want to develop if you plan on attracting a woman of substance.*

The Ability To Trump The Intimacy Card- *When you meet a woman, do not put her on a pedestal simply because you think she is attractive or because you want to get physically intimate with her. Even if that is your reason for talking to her it is best if your actions or words do not convey that reality at least not for now. You should carry yourself as if getting physically intimate with her is not your main goal, let her know that you love physical intimacy with the right female but that is not the most important thing that you are looking for, play hard to get. Tease her but never initiate anything beyond what she initiates first. If she is attracted to you in a physical way she will let you know it even if it's subtle. By not putting too much emphasis on physical intimacy this will drive her crazy and she will practically throw the intimacy on you at some point. Behave as if it's not that big a deal as if you can get that from a female anytime. It is far better to seduce her mind first before trying to seduce her body. Don't distance yourself from intimacy too far or she will think you are just not interested in her. The Christian voice in me keeps telling me to tell you gentleman to "love God's creation but sin not." Ok I said it. Now back to what I was* *saying, do not put the "candy box" or the female on a pedestal that is above and beyond where they both deserve to be if it means that you have to lower yourself and your values to get closer to either one.*

Honesty And Truth- *Contrary to popular belief, women can handle the truth. They may or may not like it but they can handle it just fine. It is in a man's nature to not be too honest with a female in the beginning because we don't want to miss out on the conquest. Truth be told, the more upfront you are about your intentions when you first meet a female the less frustrating the whole interaction will be. You should just be honest about what you really want from a female and let her decide if she wants to deal with you and give you the chance to get it. There is a term that is used these days and is practiced quite often. The term is called "friends with benefits." Some people don't like that term due to the connotation and pre-conceived notions that comes with being a "friend with benefits." Whether you agree with the practice or not, the positive thing about that type of relationship is the fact that both parties are pretty upfront about what they want from each other and what they expect. If you know that you are a playa and you don't want to settle down with just one female just be honest and let the female know. Tell her "hey I'm digging you right now but I'm not ready to settle down and get into anything serious. Here, put your phone number in my phone and I will call you later this evening or tomorrow to let you know about an event that I will be attending that I think you would enjoy attending as my guest." Keep it simple, honest and walk away. If she is feeling your vibe and she is interested she will let you know soon enough.*

Know Where You're Going And Why- *I heard a female on a radio interview say that there is nothing more captivating than to watch a man that knows where he is going and has a plan of how he's going to get there. The female also stated that it is even more intoxicating when a female is riding with him on that journey and she is not sure where he is going but the landmarks and her internal GPS assures her that he is headed in the right direction. The signs along the way also reveal to her that he is taking her somewhere that she is going to enjoy. As a man you should always be going somewhere. Laying around with no purpose or sense of direction is not an option. If you are a Man and you have a wife or children or other people that depend on you then you should always be going somewhere or planning out what your next move is going to be. You should always be going somewhere and heading in that direction. Your woman will follow you to just about anywhere if she's convinced that you know where you're going and more importantly why you're going there. Once she can see the benefits of following you and that the benefits are worth the ride, you will become like gold to her very valuable. Be a man of focus, a man of goals and a man of direction. Even if you are not quite sure where you're going, pick a nice destination along the way to aim for.*

Be The Best Bum You Can Be- *I am fully aware that no matter what you read in this book and no matter what advice is given there will be at least one of you that will decide that you aren't going to do anything that's going to uplift or upgrade your life. You have made the conscious decision that you are going to be a bum. If you have made that decision then please be the best bum you can be. If you're going to be a bum there are a few things that you need to be doing. Keep your momma's or girlfriend's house clean at all times since you will obviously have a lot of spare time on your hands. Learn to cook, nobody eats better than a bum because you are always eating somebody else's food. Read a few books on massage therapy so that you can give your lady a decent massage when she gets home from working all day. Keep your momma's car and your lady's car nice and clean as you are probably driving it more than she is. If you're going to be a bum you need to learn to pray real good for at least 30 seconds. Pray that you fail at being a bum and pray that God will cloth you not in Gucci or Versace but pray that God cloth you in your right mind. After you get through saying that prayer, Thank God for creating people foolish enough to let you live out your dreams of being bum at their expense. If you're going to be a bum please take daily showers and brush your teeth and hair. If you're going to be a bum at least be funny and have a sense of humor, that way you can at least brighten up the sad situation you're in. If you're going to be the best bum you can be Please recognize that you are a bum and ask for help to get you out of that category. If you do all of these things you will become a better bum guaranteed. If any of you bums out there are offended by this section then there is one way you can deal with it. Don't be a bum. Please do not confuse being down on your luck with the term bum. Anyone can find themselves down and out at some point in life but a bum sometimes purposely chooses to be a bum and he aspires to be nothing more or nothing less.*

Tips For Married Men That Will Make Your Wife More Interested In You

Always Be Caught Doing More Than She Does – *A friend of mine from college asked me one day what was the secret to keeping your wife happy and having her remain attracted to you. One of the first things I told him was to always be caught doing more for her than she does for you. If she cooks tell her how good her cooking is and clean the kitchen and dishes afterwards. If you see her cleaning go clean something too. Clean something big like the closets or attic or her car. If all else fails go out in the garage and start building something. It could be anything. Go out and hammer on some wood or run a chain saw in the back yard. You must let her see you sweat. Make some noise with some tools, drop a few things. Sound really busy and try to look like you know what you're doing. Anytime a woman see you working with a circular saw or cutting pieces of wood, as soon as she hear that sound and see that cut wood hit the ground with sawdust flying she is convinced you are a Man and know what you are doing. She will go back in the house thinking to herself that you are really building something. She doesn't know what you are building but it looks like you are building something. If she ask you what it is don't tell her. Tell her it's a surprise and that she will know as soon as you are finished. Get under a car and get greasy even if you don't know what you're doing. Get a good ratchet set and wrenches and just unscrew and screw in and out some bolts. The greasier, blacker and sweatier you get the more it looks like you know what you are doing. Get them hands dirty and look like a man that's fixing something or building something important that will help the family. You are not trying to trick her because in the end you better have something to show for that little dog and pony show you just performed. The key is to always find ways to look and actually be busier building your future and a better future for her and your kids.*

Help Her Achieve Her Dreams and Goals – *Find out what your wife's goals and dreams are and then help her achieve them. Be supportive of her goals and help provide her with the knowledge and resources to make it happen. When you ask her what her goals are make sure the goals that you help her with are goals that she has set for herself, not goals for the family or her relationship. These should be her own individual personal goals that are for her benefit and development as her own individual person. Help her achieve these goals and find ways to celebrate each time one of her goals is realized. Take her out to a nice park and just walk and talk about what she* wants out of life and how you can assist her in making her dreams a reality. She will develop a deeper and more meaningful respect for you. You will find that in this case the more you help her to reach her goals the more she will help you reach yours.

Be Positive And Uplifting- You should always be a source of positive energy for your wife. No matter what situation you find yourself in always find something positive in it and remain positive throughout it. You need to be sensitive to the situation but always be a source of uplift for your wife when she needs it most. When you see that your wife is feeling down grab her hand and take her for a nice ride, stop by dairy queen and get her some ice cream or go sit on a bench near water. It could be a waterfall, a lake, a fountain in the mall or take her on a weekend trip to the beach. It's something soothing and relaxing about being around water.

Be Decisive And Lead- You must be a leader in your marriage and family. A woman loves a man that knows how to lead. You must know how to lead yourself, your family and your marriage. There is a huge difference between leading and controlling the relationship. When you lead she will want to follow you because she knows that you know where you are going and she wants to go there with you. You need to be the type of leader where if you were to say to her "get the kids and all of you go get in the car, we're going to the local crack house to get dinner and some tickets to see Tupac live at Carowinds". You should be the type of leader where she will be out in the car with the kids waiting on you before you finish your sentence because she trusts your leadership that much. Ok we all know that Tupac is probably dead or at the very least no longer living in Harlem but your lady better act like he's alive and she's going to ride with you to Smitty's crack and smack house to get them tickets. You should be a man of decisions and leadership.

Pray With And For Your Wife- There is nothing more powerful as a man than being a spiritual leader in your home and marriage. When things are going good you should pray. When things are going bad you should pray. Prayer is the glue that keeps your relationship and foundation strong. Don't be afraid to take your wife by the hand and pray for her and with her at anytime. Some of the roughest and toughest times in your marriage will require that you pray together if you're going to make it through those times. Your wife will never object to you praying for her and your family. Become a man of prayer.

Make A Recording Of Her favorite Songs- *Make a list of 15 of your wife's favorite songs and have them burned onto a cd. Put that cd in her car so that she can listen to it on her way to work, to the grocery store or anytime she is in the car. This is a simple gesture but it is worth its weight in gold.*

Ask Her Is There anything You Can Do To Make Her Day Better- *This is a simple phrase that you can use to let your wife know that you care about her. When you say it mean it. She will look at you in a whole new light if she is not used to being asked this question. Use it as often as possible. Most of the time when you ask your wife this she will say there is nothing you can do, but offer to do something anyway. I have found out that no woman will turn down a nice foot massage or shoulder massage at the end of a long day.*

Give Her A Chance To Miss You- *They say absence makes the heart grow fonder. This is especially true if your absence is the result of you going away to do something to better yourself or your marriage and family. When two people live together under one roof for an extended period of time it is to your benefit to take a break and get away every now and then to rejuvenate your mind, body and spirit. You should create opportunities to spend some time away from the relationship with yourself to just enjoy being you. Find a hobby that you enjoy that you can do by yourself without having your wife or family around. Go on a fishing trip, get on your motorcycle and ride on a scenic route just to enjoy the scenery. Volunteer to go on a business trip for a few days. Relationships and marriage can be mentally and emotionally draining at times and being able to get away for a weekend of relaxation and just sleeping in a bed all by yourself can re-energize you mentally and physically. Don't be afraid to give your relationship some breathing room as your wife will appreciate the time away from you as well. Give your wife a chance to miss you and appreciate what you bring to her life.*

Be An Active Father In Your Children's Life- *Your role as a father is greater than any role that you could ever have. Your wife understands this and appreciates you when you assume your fatherly responsibilities. A woman's children are extremely important to her and how you treat them is just as important. Spend as much quality time with your children as possible and be comfortable in your role as a father. Take your children on vacation, take them to explore the world, introduce them to new and exciting experiences. Time flies by so fast and before you know it your children will be grown and gone. Pray with and for your children and give them a strong spiritual foundation that will last them a life time. Be the best father that you can be and strive to become an active part of your children's lives.*

Have Goals And Dreams That You Are Working On- *Not only is it important for you as a man to help your lady achieve her goals and dreams but you should also have some attainable goals and dreams for yourself that will help you further your mission as a man. Set goals and dreams for yourself that will benefit not only yourself but those around you. You should be a man that knows where he's going and how he's going to get there. You should be constantly working on making your goals and dreams a reality by working on them a little every day until you find yourself having accomplished them. Most of the things you will accomplish in life will start with having a goal or a dream. Always be working on making your dreams to become a reality. Life is far more exciting when you have a definite purpose or dream that you are working on or working towards.*

Tips For The College Man That Will Make Women More Interested In You

Create A Money Making Hustle On Campus- *Some of the most financially challenging times in your life will be when you are in college. College students tend to not have paying jobs that provide extra spending money. Most of the jobs that college students have are exclusively for helping to pay their tuition to stay in school. When you are a college man on campus and you have disposable income to spend on things like dates, clothes, restaurants, weekend getaways then your stock rises very high in the eyes of the women, providing that everything else about you is on point as well. When you have a good money making hustle you develop all types of skills that make you more attractive. As a hustler you learn to use your communication skills to get what you want, you become more interpersonal, your confidence increases, you can be more adventurous and you develop business skills that can serve you no matter where you go. Being a hustler is especially attractive to women if you're selling something that they want. Sell hotdogs in the dorm, write term papers on the weekends, start a car taxi service or become a physical fitness trainer. Do anything that's legal and can make you some disposable income. In this digital age it is easier now than ever to start an online business overnight and start making money immediately. You don't have to make a lot of money for women to notice you and to become attracted to you. Be creative and business minded enough to make enough money to take them out to a nice inexpensive night out or to buy you some nice eye catching cloths that compliments your physique. $50 is the magic number on a college campus. A man shouldalways have a minimum of $50 dollars at all times as this will generally suffice to handle most of your inexpensive dating needs while in college.*

Provide Massage Therapy Sessions In Your Dorm Room – *When I was in college, I created a massage therapy business called PleasureDome Inc. The purpose of PleasureDome was to provide relaxation therapy sessions for stressed out college girls in a relaxing, safe, private and inviting environment. I had the red light, the red silk sheets and pillows, soft jazz, slow jams playing in the background, candles, lotions, oils, heart shaped balloons floating on the ceiling, box of chocolate candies and a refrigerator full of fruity beverages and plastic champagne glasses. You could only experience PleasureDome by invitation only and that is only if a previous "client" had recommended you. Discretion was advised at all times even though you fully knew that the females were going to run back and tell at least two of their friends about the experience. I charged $2 per female for a 15 minute massage and advertisement was by word of mouth only. During the week of exams or major testing my clientele grew and more than doubled. Needless to say I was quite popular at least in my mind with the ladies on campus and it did wonders for my interpersonal skills and confidence interacting with the females on campus. Coincidently I met my future wife while I was in college as a result of PleasureDome. She came to my dorm with a friend of hers not to get a massage but just to walk her female friend to my dorm to meet someone else. I saw her and quickly went over to her to introduce myself. She wasn't interested in me at all as she had heard about me being the proprietor and owner of "Pleasure Dumb" as she called it. I told her that I would shut PleasureDome down completely if she went out with me. 2 weeks later I shut down my little operation, sold the concept and my entire inventory to one of my friends for $50. I took $30 of that money and bought my then future wife several packs of hair weave and she started doing braids on campus. She turned that $30 into $150 in one weekend and she continued to make money the whole time we were in college. I ended up marrying her, she is CJ's Mom.*

***Warning-creating a PleasureDome may get you expelled from college**

Develop A Nice Physique- *Get in shape and try to develop the best physique that you can. The best way to start developing a nice physique is to immediately start working out and trimming down your stomach. Getting rid of your belly fat is the quickest and most efficient way to start to develop the type of body that is attractive. Find a famous person that has the type of physique that you aspire to obtain and use that person as your body role model.*

Guard Your Reputation At All Cost- *When you are on a college campus and you are dealing with females, word travels fast of any and every encounter that you have with women on your campus .There is no such thing as discretion when you are in college. Even though everyone has sworn to a code of secrecy you can be sure that before you leave any situation or encounter, the word has already started to circulate about what you did or* didn't do. Be sure to not engage in any activity or encounter that can be detrimental to your reputation. As a man on a college campus please do not engage in any activities with a female not unless you are 100% sure that the word that will be generated afterwards will enhance your reputation and not erode it. Many a college man's reputation has gone down in flames simply because he thought what was done in the dark stayed in the dark. When I was in college there was a saying, "Don't touch what you can't handle and don't ask for what you can't afford." Your reputation on a college campus is one of your most valuable assets and your stock can rise or fall on any given day. Whatever you do or get ready to do, ask yourself the question, "if what I'm about to do will be broadcast all over campus the next day, will this decision increase or decrease my reputation." To borrow a phrase from an old Bartle and Jaymes wine commercial; "Serve no wine until it's time."

Be Bold And Mysterious- *When you're on a college campus the bravado, boldness and competition is at an all-time high. Catching the attention of the college girls is not something you do by accident you have to make a deliberate attempt to catch the eye and interest of the female that you desire. You are on a campus with a lot of other guys with swagger, looks, money, nice physiques and mouth pieces that can sell ice to an Eskimo and you can't afford to just blend into the background. Doing something bold and interesting to stand out is almost mandatory if you don't stand out already. You could join a fraternity, run for class president by running a unique and eye catching campaign or just be a man of mystery only giving the women an occasional glimpse of what you have to offer. You must arouse their curiosity and make them notice you. Let the women know that you are interesting and bold but don't let them know too much. Make it a habit to know way more about them than they know about you. The reason for this is that once a woman knows all about you then you will become less of a challenge and boring to her. Be the carrot dangling on a string that keeps make her wanting to get closer and closer to you to find out what you are all about.*

Go To Class And Learn As Much As Possible- *As a man on a college campus you must always remember your primary reason for being there is to get an education and get a degree. Getting the right degree can help you to get an interesting job that pays well and provides you with the resources to get everything that you want in life including a nice home, nice cars and attractive women. When you stay focused on that goal while you are in school the women will start looking at you as a potential future mate. Take advantage of internships as graduation comes quickly and a lot of college women meet their future husbands while in college. By the time you reach your senior year you will have women checking for you hard if you have done what it takes to set yourself apart and prepared yourself well for the next stage in life.*

Tips For Fathers That Will Make Your Children Interested In You

Give them discipline- *One of the greatest gifts you can give your children as a father is the gift of discipline. Discipline is not just you chastising or punishing your child for negative behavior or actions but discipline is teaching them a character trait that will serve them well in all areas of life. When I think of the word discipline in the context of fatherhood I think of it this way; discipline is simply teaching your child to do the things that they got to do, when they really don't want to do it so that they can do the things that they really want to do in the future. We as fathers like to spoil our children and we will jump through hoops to make sure that they have a better life than we did. Along with us coddling and rewarding our children we must always teach them discipline. Discipline will keep them from straying too far off of the right path and it will give them the focus and drive to accomplish in life the things that they wish to accomplish. Your child's degree of self- discipline will be a great asset to them and as a father you must teach it to them as early as possible. They will thank you for it later.*

Listen to them- important to girls and your daughters- *As a father it is very important that you pause from your speeches, war stories and determination to show your son who's the boss to be quiet sometimes and just listen to him. You will be amazed at how much you find out about your son good and bad by just stopping and just listening to him and what he is really saying to you. With so many things competing with your children's time, mind and attention it is important more than ever to connect with your child by really listening to them and understanding where they are coming from. With daughters in particular you don't really have to say as much; as listening is what she desires from you the most. She needs for you to make her feel important and accepted, Just nod your head to let her know you are still listening and always be willing to give good sound advice at the appropriate time. Sometimes the best thing you can do as a father is to know when to be quiet and listen.*

Don't Try To Turn Your Children Into Mini Clones Of You- *My first FaceBook post I ever wrote was a post on the day my son CJ turned 13 years old. My post was about how we should not try so hard to make our children clones of our ideas or views of the world. We should allow our children to develop into their own individual selves and with their own thoughts and goals and we should be the voice that they hear in the back of their mind when they are unsure about where to go or what to do next. We should be a guiding voice and helping hand in assisting in the shaping and molding of our children and helping them to be who they wish to be and who they were born to be.*

Love And Show Affection Toward Their Mother- *The family is the most important structure in a child's life. The ideal family consists of a mother and a father and all the siblings living under one happy roof. While this was the norm at one time this family dynamic is becoming more rare as time goes by. As a father it is absolutely crucial that you show love, respect and affection toward their mother as this will shape how they relate to men and women in the future. If your children grow up in a loving family then they will tend to be more loving individuals. You should never disrespect, show hate or make disparaging remarks about your children's mother in their presence. Show affection and let your children see what a healthy loving relationship looks like. How a young boy sees his father treat his mother will have an impact on how he treats girls and women in the future. How a young girl sees her father treat her mother will give her an idea and a sense of how she thinks she should be treated by boys and men in the future. While no one can be the perfect father you should always take into account what messages you are sending to your children during every encounter or situation that they see you interacting in.*

Romantic Date Ideas For $20 And Under

The Prince If I Was Your Girlfriend Date- *In the late 1980's a popular musical artist named Prince released a song called "If I Was Your Girlfriend." The song was a weird salacious hit. In the song Prince sung about becoming his girlfriend's girlfriend. At first it didn't make much sense but as the song went on it gave a blue print for an inexpensive intimate date and how to get a female to completely fall for you. The date ideas that could be gotten from this song is as follows: Pick your lady up and Drive her to her next hair appointment to get her hair done, Drive her to go shopping and help her pick out her cloths, Drive her to a park and walk and listen to her talk about whatever is bothering her and get her to talk about her past hurts. (talking about past hurts is a Jedi mind trick that is known to make women feel closer to you as they will look to you to make the pain go away) cooking her breakfast, taking a bath or shower together with clothes on of course. Notice I said Drive her to do these things not Pay for her to do these things. All of these things she already do, she just do them with her girlfriend. Become her girlfriend for the day* and the only thing you will be paying for is gas in your car which is already paid for. You can keep the $20 and enjoy all the benefits of a unique and casual date that ends with you taking a nice relaxing bubble bath and cooking breakfast in the morning. The key to the bubble bath or shower is to promise to not try to do anything beyond just taking the shower or bubble bath and that it's for relaxation purposes only. You will find that it is easier to pull this date off than you think. All you have to do is tell her what you're going to do and do it. This is for mature adult Men only!!

The Romantic Dollar Store and Ice Cream Date- *Take your date to a mall that has a dollar store in it. Go into the dollar store and buy 5 stuffed teddy bears at $1 each and 5 small gift bags to put the teddy bears in. Take the teddy bears and you and your date just walk through the mall and see if you can find 5 couples to give the teddy bears to. This is a fun date idea and you will get the chance to meet other interesting couples as you give them the teddy bears and tell them why you gave it to them. Trust me when I tell you that your date is going to be impressed with your creativity and your willingness to give her the opportunity to meet other couples. You can arrange to hang out sometimes with some of the happy couples that you meet throughout the date if you find them to be the type of people that you wouldn't mind hanging out with. After you two have enjoyed meeting new people and giving them the gift of the teddy bears, go to a nice ice cream shop in the mall and sit down and buy yourselves some ice cream to eat. It's something about eating ice cream that makes you feel better about life. After eating the ice cream you can walk through the mall or you can sit and people watch and laugh and have a good time. As simple as this date sounds it will have a lasting effect on not only her but also on the other couples that you meet. She will be talking about that date to her friends long after it's over.* **Cost:** *$5 for the bears,* **$2.50** *for the bags and* **$10** *for the ice cream.* **Total cost $17.50** *plus tax.*

The Romantic Shop & Drop Date- *Take your date to an upscale mall in your area. Open the car door for her and hold her hand as you walk through the mall. Take her to a greeting card store and tell her that you two are to pick out a nice greeting card for each other that best describes how you feel about your relationship at the moment. Each one of you should pick out a card without the other one seeing which card you picked out. Put the cards in an envelope and exchange them right there in the store. Both of you read your cards and when you're finished reading them put them back on the shelf where you got them from. Walk out of the store holding hands free to discuss why you picked out the card that you chose. Continue to walk through the mall and tell your date that if today was your one year anniversary of being boyfriend and girlfriend what gift would she get for you. Tell her that you will give her 15 minutes to go in a store of her choosing to pick the gift out. Tell her to text you when she has found the gift so that you can come see what she had chosen for you. When she texts you, go to the store that she is in and let her hand you the gift that she has chosen for you. Thank her for the gift and place it back on the shelf where she found it.*

Hold her hand and walk out of the store and feel free to discuss the gift she chose for you. Now it's your turn to do the same thing for her. After you both have exchanged gifts and placed them back onto the shelves walk through the mall holding hands. Walk your date back to your car and start driving back to your place. Stop by the Red Box and pick up a good movie then stop by Little Caesars and pick up a $5 dollar pizza, some seasoned wings and her favorite non-alcoholic beverage and take her to your place and enjoy. Give her a complimentary back massage to end the date.

Cost: $0.00 for *cards, gifts, massage,* **$1.50** *for movie,* $15 *for food.* **Total cost $17.50** *+tax.*

The Top Of The Tower Date- *When my wife and I were first married and we had our son CJ I was the only one working for a little over a year. Needless to say that our funds were a little tight and we were on a strict budget. For valentine's day that year I wanted to treat my wife to a nice evening at a nice restaurant but I needed to stay within our budget. (the word budget is just a nice way of saying we were broke) I told my wife to get dressed up real nice and that I was taking her out for a night of dining, romance and fun. She knew about the "budget" so I caught her completely by surprise. Upon leaving the house to begin our night out on the town I pulled up to Burger King and I bought two of our favorite sandwiches and I asked for two courtesy cups of water. We received our "sammiches" as they are called when you're really hungry and we headed on our way. We ate them sammiches as we were riding along and I headed for downtown. As I drove my wife kept asking me where were we going and I kept telling her it was a surprise. As we made our way downtown I pulled into the parking deck of the trendiest building in the city that we were living in at the time. The building was over 50 stories high with upscale retail stores, architect firms and art galleries. At the top of this building was an upscale restaurant that was called The Top Of The Towers. It was an exclusive restaurant located on the 50th floor which was at the top of the building overlooking the city's beautiful skyline.*

The Top Of The Towers required reservations at least a week in advance and they were slammed pack as it was Valentine's day. I opened the car door for my wife as she stepped out and she asked me again where are we going. I told her it was a surprise. We went inside the building, stepped into the elevator and I hit the button for the 50th floor. My wife was a little concerned because she saw on the elevator wall directory that the only thing on the 50th floor was the Top Of The Towers restaurant. Before we reached the floor where I was determined to make my dream come true I told her to not say a word just to follow my lead. We reached the 50th floor and the elevator doors opened and there standing in front of us was the grand entrance to one of the most exclusive restaurants in the city. I held my wife's hand as I confidently walked up to the reservation station. I said "We have reservations for two and the hostess that made our reservation last week stated that we would be able to get a window seat on the east wing of the restaurant." The hostess at the reservation station asked me my name and I told her and she looked up and down the reservation list two or three times looking for something that I knew she wasn't going to find, which was our names on that reservation list. She stated "I'm sorry I can't seem to find your name on the list." I started to chuckle and I said "you're funny please check it again, this is the second time this year that the restaurant has mysteriously lost my reservation." She said "oh you've eaten here before?" I said yes my business client and I have eaten here a few times. She asked me my name again and then she said I'm sorry we don't have your reservation.

At this point my wife said let's just leave. I said No we're not leaving because I have been planning this for over a month and I'm not going to let this ruin our evening because someone made a mistake. I then said to the hostess, "I specifically asked for a window seat on the east part of the restaurant when I made the reservation and now you're telling me that you lost my reservation." The hostess again apologized and I told her that I wanted to speak to general manager of the establishment because this was just ridiculous. She said that the general manager was not in the restaurant that he was out of town but she could let me speak to a manger. I quickly then said look, I don't know what you all did with my reservation but I will tell you what, "I'm willing to compromise and just take two seats at the bar on the west side of the building as we are tired of waiting for you to find our reservation." The hostess said ok and escorted us to the bar where we were seated and she apologized.

Disclaimer: I asked God to forgive me for being dishonest in that situation at that time but here is how this whole $20 dollar upscale date went down. I never made reservations to the Top Of The Towers as there was no way I could afford the $200 that it costs for two people to eat a meal in that place. I knew that they prided themselves on their customer service and reputation and I also knew that I really wanted to be on the west side of the restaurant by the bar from the very beginning because that side of the building is all glass and you are on the 50th floor surrounded by glass and the ambiance was spectacular even while sitting at the bar. The bar was just fine with me but I knew that they were going to move us to a table as soon as possible due to our "lost reservation." We were quickly escorted from the bar to a romantic little table for two up against the window on the 50th floor of the most exclusive restaurant in the city on Valentine's day. The tables were already decorated with candles, flowers and complimentary chocolate candies as the tables come standard with these little extras. They automatically bring you a complimentary basket of artisan bread, dipping oil and a pitcher of water. I asked for a dessert menu as I explained that we had already eaten earlier and we ordered a large serving of cheesecake which was more than enough for two people and we listened to the live band playing romantic music and my wife and I laughed and talked and conversed with other couples in the restaurant and we had a good time. We saw the hostess on our way out of the restaurant and she again apologized and asked us to come back. I told her I would but I would make sure to call before I arrived to ensure that they have my reservation. I told you in the beginning we were on a budget and here is the final cost. Parking *$0.00* validated from the hostess, Cheesecake, Artisan bread & water-*$12.50,* candles, chocolates & flowers -*$0.00,* tips- *$4.00* which was 32% of our total bill. Total cost plus tax approx. *$18.50*

Fun Christian Date Ideas For $20 And Under

Thrift-Store Marathon-*Basically you map out a bunch of thrift stores in your area and visit each one and look for bargains. This is really fun when you have a specific treasure or item that you are looking for. Cost;* *$20.00* *budget.*

Garage Sale Shopping-*Similar to the thrift-store marathon, you just spend a couple hours hitting up garage sales. Set a* *$20* *budget and see who can find the best merchandise.*

Visit Display Homes-*I always love visiting new display homes and open houses as they give you a chance to dream or plan for your next move! Cost* *$0.00*

Test Drive-*Visit car dealerships and test drive some of your favorite luxury and sport cars. Cost* *$0.00*

Movie Night- *Head over to the red box and pick up 3 good movies for a movie marathon evening. Find some classics that you haven't seen before . All You need is a blanket, popcorn, and your favorite beverages. Cost* *$15.00*

Get Cooking-*One of you make the other's favorite meal, and the other one make the other's favorite dessert. Then enjoy them both together. Listen to some good music as you cook. Cost:* **$20.00** *budget.*

Re-Arrange- *Give each other a room in your house to redesign or rearrange. Something as simple as re-arranging the furniture in the rooms or adding different lighting or artwork makes for an interesting date. Cost:* **$20.00** *budget.*

 See The Great Outdoors-*Head over to* <u>*localhikes.com*</u> *and find a trail near you and go hiking. This is a great outdoor date that often facilitates great conversation. Cost:* **$10.00**

Biking- *If you already have a bike, start riding together. If you don't have one there are many places that will rent them to you. Cost:* **$0.00**

Stargazing-*If it is a cloudless night, you could head to the library and find some astronomy books. Find out which constellations are showing and look for them in the sky. Grab a cozy blanket and enjoy laying under the stars together. Cost:$* **0:00**

Videos On Women, Relationships And Dating

Pause right here and listen to at least two songs and watch at least one video below on Youtube before continuing,

Make Me A Believer –Luther Vandross-   Song

Rain   – SWV -   Song

This Very Moment –KCi & JoJo-   Song

After The Dance- Marvin Gaye -   Song

How To Attract Women –Stephan Erdman-   Video

Self Confidence–Stephan Erdman-   Video

Caution In Courtship Dating –TD Jakes-   Video

Before You Say I Do To Marriage –TD Jakes- Video

5 Reasons You Are Not Successful With Women- Video

Book Note Page For You To Write Down Ways You Will Become More Desirable

Chapter 5

<u>"Use Your Body To Your Advantage"</u>

I was in one of my favorite clothing stores recently and as I was perusing the aisles I came across one of the coolest looking shirts that I had ever seen. It was an Italian fitted dress shirt with a solid white collar and the rest of the shirt had colored vertical stripes with white sleeve cuffs. It was the perfect shirt for a guy with an athletic physique. I proceeded to take the shirt to the dressing room to try it on just imagining how good it was going to look on me. I went into the dressing room and took off my shirt to try on the new shirt and as soon as I turned my back to the door and to look in the mirror and BAM just that quick I was robbed. Yes robbed in the clothing store. Someone had robbed me of my 6 pack. I looked in the mirror in disbelief, shock and Awe. As I stood there staring at the part of my body where my 6 pack used to reside I felt an overwhelming sense of loss. Me being the man that I am I did what most men would do in a situation like that, I look in the mirror and took a deep breath and held my stomach in. I exhaled after a few seconds and I took another deep breath and held my stomach in again this time a little longer. I started to get dizzy so I exhaled. I took another deep breath for the third time and held it in as long as I could and I started to get woozy. At that moment I looked at myself in the mirror and I said to myself "what are you doing, who are you trying to fool." As I stood there looking in the mirror it became abundantly clear that I had robbed myself and the mirror convicted me and freed me at the same time.

The mirror had convicted me because it showed me the physical and mental condition that I was in but it also freed me because I was no longer in denial and it showed me the areas in my physical and mental state that I needed to work on. That mirror experience was a wakeup call for me and it brought back memories of a time when I was in peak physical condition and my mind was right. As a former athlete back in the day I prided myself on my physique and I never passed up an opportunity to hit the weights, get sweaty, put on my tight tank top and walk around like I was God's gift to humanity. My body was one of my greatest assets as far as I was concerned and when I took a real hard glance in the mirror that day I knew that if I was to ever become physically healthy again that I needed to start by immediately taking better care of myself. The way you look and feel will have a direct and correlating affect on how successful you can be in all areas of your life.

Teach your sons that to be at your best and operate at your peak level you must become and remain physically and mentally fit. One of the gifts that come with being a man is your physical strength and prowess. This strength and prowess is a necessary attribute that you must have as a man if you are going to walk in your role and purpose as a man. If you lose your strength or your mental ability to function as you were designed to function in this society, the consequences can and will be detrimental to your survival as a man. Taking of yourself physically is an absolute necessity as its tangible benefits are numerous and adherence to this truth is required to sustain and maintain the lifestyle that you desire. Physical and Mental conditioning is not an option it is a must. You are never too old or too young to improve your physical health and the best time to start is now.

Tips To Help Maintain Peak Physical Conditioning

Obtain A Complete Physical And Evaluation- *don't be afraid to visit your primary care physician and advise them of your desire to maintain peak physical and mental fitness. They will advise you of what you need to do. You should get at minimum a yearly physical.*

Develop A Regular Physical Fitness Routine- *As a young male athletics will more than likely play a big part in your physical development. exercise regularly including walking, running, cardio, weight training, or any physical activity that will cause you to become in better physical conditioning. Join a fitness center, walking club, participate in high energy sports.*

Maintain Healthy Food Choices- *eat healthier, fruits, vegetables, whole grains, alkaline water, coconut water and foods. Obtain the services of a nutritionist.*

Have A Vision Of The Type Of Physique You Wish To Have- *aspire to developing a certain type of physique. Find a person that has the type of body that you wish to have and aspire to it.*

Stay Hydrated And Drink Plenty Of Water- *water flushes out undesired toxins in your body, helps create clearer skin, and energizes your body cells.*

Buy Cloths That Are A Size Or Two Too Small- *find an outfit that you really like and buy it in a size smaller than you are now. This will aid in motivating you to trim down.*

The Benefits Of Maintaining Peak Physical Conditioning

Helps keep the heart healthy - *Your heart is a muscle. In fact it's one of the most critical muscles in your body because it controls the flow of blood around your system. In itself it's like a pumping station — the right side bringing in blood from your body and pumping it to your lungs, and the left side bringing in blood from the lungs and pumping it to the rest of your body. Continuous and sustained exercise can help to condition the heart and lungs. When you exercise you breath faster and the heart pumps more blood throughout your body. Your blood provides your body with oxygen and important nutrients, while at the same time carrying harmful waste products out of your body. Regular physical activity can help to reduce the risk of heart disease.*

Makes you feel good and reduces stress- *Want a natural high? Try a little exercise! Whenever you exercise your brain releases a natural chemical called endorphins which make you feel good. The release of these endorphins is the natural method that you're body uses to regulate feelings of pain and hunger. A widely publicized observation is the supposed "runner's high." Here the person who is doing continuous and demanding exercise will eventually reach a threshold that stimulates the release of endorphin production. As endorphins are released into our bloodstream they also help to improve our mood. Have you ever noticed how good you've felt after exercising? Well that's a combination of the endorphins released in your body along with the sense of achievement for doing the exercise. Studies have also shown that those endorphins play an important part in reducing stress and helping us to relax.*

Weight loss-ature*Not only does exercise keep your heart healthy and make you feel good, but it also helps keep those extra pounds off. Often those who are overweight have a slower metabolism than those who are leaner. And scientifically it has been proven that those who have lean muscle tone burn fat even more efficiently. Consistent cardiovascular exercise, 3 or 4 times a week, helps to burn fat and convert it into lean muscle. The best way to burn fat is to do aerobic exercise like running, jogging and cycling. Anaerobic exercises (like weightlifting) do not focus on burning fat but help to build muscles. But the muscles in turn compliment the aerobic exercises as bigger muscles help to burn more calories.*

Stronger immune system-text*When you exercise your immune systems gets a temporary boost in the production of macrophages. These are the cells that attack bacteria. Your body temperature also rises which helps to fight off germs. Generally moderate exercise is very good for the immune system because it helps to strengthen and stimulate the immune system. For high intensity exercises such as marathon running enough rest and recovery time is required to prevent a negative effect being sustained on the immune system.*

Reduces risk of cancer- *Many studies support the use of regular exercise in the prevention and treatment of cancer. One such study carried out by the Cancer Research Foundation analyzed the results of more than 50 separate studies into bowel cancer. It found that people who exercised regularly were less likely to develop bowel cancer. Exercises as simple as manual work, hiking and gardening all are activities that count as positive measure towards the prevention of cancer.*

Reduces blood pressure-*Exercise can help to reduce resting blood pressure in people who have hypertension by an average of 10 points. The best exercises include walking, jogging, cycling, swimming and rowing. Millions of Americans have high blood pressure. High blood pressure can lead to heart attacks, strokes, and kidney failure if left untreated. For those who do have high blood pressure it is wise to consult a doctor about the best of action for exercising.*

Increases productivity and energy levels-*Your nutrition, sleeping habits and stress levels all affect your energy levels. But exercise is a sure way to help increase energy and stamina and help to make you more alert. As you exercise, you increase your heart rate causing more blood to flow around your body and through your brain. The oxygen from your blood which your brain is now receiving is absorbed by the brain cells making you feel more energetic and mentally alert. Because blood also contains glucose which your brain uses as fuel, exercise increases the glucose levels received by the brain and also enhances the ability of the enzymes in your body to use that fuel.*

The following workout routine is a good routine to begin to get in really good physical condition from a physique standpoint. The goal is to complete each workout routine straight through with as little breaks in between as possible. Upon completion of the routines you will feel invincible and ready to conquer the world.

THE SIMPLE SPARTAN 300 WORKOUT ROUTINE

Jumping Jacks -	25
Dumbbell curls right arm-	25
Dumbbell curls left arm -	25
Ab Crunches -	25
Sit ups-	25
Pushups -	25
Core rotations -	25
Forward Arm Rotations	25
Backward Arm Rotations	25
Fast 50 jumping jacks-	50
Fast 25 pushups -	25

THE INTERMEDIATE 300 WORKOUT

Sit ups	50
Dumbbell curls right arm	50
Dumbbells curls left arm	50
Pushups -	50
Body Squats & Jumps -	50
Ab Crunches -	50

THE ADVANCED 300 WORKOUT

Pushups –	100
Sit ups	100
Ab Crunches	100

Videos On Maintaining Physical And Mental Fitness
Pause here and watch at least one video below

5 Principles Of Muscle Building –Elliot Hulse-
YouTube

The Strongest Version Of Yourself –Elliot Hulse
YouTube

Exercises That Eliminate Fear –Elliot Hulse-
YouTube

P90X Workout-
YouTube

Chapter 6

<u>"5 Tools Every Man Must Have In His Tool Box"</u>

I was talking to an older gentleman one day and he was talking about how he wished that he was young again so that he could go back and redo some of the things in his life. The older gentleman stated that he felt like that he did not live up to his true potential. I asked him what did he meant by living up to his true potential and most of the things he stated were related to obtaining a certain status in life or a certain position or obtaining certain assets. Most of what this gentleman was talking about was living up to the expectations that he had of himself and that he felt unfulfilled because the picture he had painted in his head of what he wanted for his life did not match his reality. I listened to the gentleman and I asked myself the question, while it is nice to obtain certain things in life as a measure of success how does one truly live up to their true potential when it appears that potential is infinite? I found myself going through the same mental self evaluation as that older gentleman and I was beating myself up just like he had done. I felt like I had not done all that I could have done to better position myself for the life of leisure, freedom and financial security that this gentleman currently had and that he was complaining about . I felt like that I had not lived up to my potential up to this point in my life according to the picture I had painted in my head.

A lot of times I was so busy going through the motions and convincing myself that I had already arrived that It kept me from really going anywhere or doing anything beyond what was my reality. Then one day it dawned on me that I would never reach my full potential if most of my accomplishments were actually lying dormant and unrealized in the corners and corridors of my own imagination. When I was talking to that older gentleman and he expressed to me his disappointment in not reaching his potential, I couldn't help but to think that he was being a little too hard on himself. It seems that he equated living up to his potential to the amount of money he had, the type of house he lived in and the professional status that he held at the time that I was speaking to him. I was listening to everything he was saying and it sounded like he did everything right as far as trying to make the best out of what he had.

He was engaging, he was kind, he was optimistic and he sounded like he was connected to those around him. He was active in his community, his church and he was living comfortably after retiring from his job after 40 years of service. By all accounts he had done everything that he could with what he had. He had taken care of his children who were all grown and doing well and he was now living the simple life of a retiree with an abundance of leisure time on his hands. He was in relatively good health and he had enough resources to travel and do pretty much whatever he wanted to do at this point in his life.

After going through that mental assessment and evaluation of my life I realized that if I wanted to take steps in the right direction of reaching my potential then I needed to start by doing one thing, which was being honest with myself. In the journey to my truth and honesty I knew that I was going to need a few things. The things that I needed were going to be the tools that guided me on my road to realizing my potential. I will now share with you some of the tools that you and your sons will need that will lead you on the road to realizing your full potential.

A Mirror- In an earlier chapter of this book I talked to you about my mirror experience and about how I looked physically when I looked in the mirror compared to how I used to look from a physique standpoint. The Powerful thing about a mirror is that it will show you where you have been, where you are now and where you have the potential to go. If you're going to reach your potential you're going to need a good mirror in your life. While an actual mirror is good to have there are other mirrors that are just as important. I went to my college homecoming awhile back and I went out with some friends to a restaurant for dinner. As we were sitting there laughing and talking and reminiscing we started talking about how most of us at the table met our significant others while we were in college. I began to tell the story of how I met my wife while in college and midway through my story my wife interrupted me and said stop lying that is not even how we met. Everyone at the table began to laugh, they were not laughing at my version of the story of how I met her but they were laughing because my wife interrupted me with such unexpected passion that it caught them off guard because they had never seen her so passionate about such a casual conversation before. My significant other was so passionate about interrupting me because she knew that I wasn't being completely honest about how we met and that my embellishments were more than she could and should bear. When she passionately interrupted me and yelled at me to stop lying she wasn't saying that because she was embarrassed by what I was saying, actually she was quite entertained by it all just like the rest of my friends at the table. My wife was passionate about interrupting me because she wanted to keep me honest and she knew that I had crossed the line between harmless embellishments and becoming an outright liar. My significant other became my mirror that day. She showed me a character flaw that I took for granted that had the potential to have repercussions on my character and reputation in the future if I didn't look at that flaw face to face and deal with it. That interaction at dinner that day showed me that my significant other was a valuable mirror that I needed. If you're going to reach your potential you are going to need people in your life that has the gift and the ability to tell you the truth about where you are and where you have the potential to go.

A Wrench- In life you are going to break some things and you will have to fix some things. In the breaking and fixing of your life you are going to need a good wrench which is an adjustable tool that when use in the right hands with the right knowledge it is able to help you fix a lot of different things. I was at a yard sale one day and there was a nice looking pool table for sale that was sitting in the garage. I went over to look at the pool table and I talked to the owner and the owner told me that it was a good pool table that the only problem with it was that one of the legs was cracked and would need to be fixed before it fell apart completely. I looked at the legs on the pool table and I convinced myself that I could fix it. The price on the pool table was a steal considering how expensive that particular model cost in the stores. Even with the broken leg the pool table was a bargain and I bought it. I took the pool table home and set it up and it it lasted for a couple of months until one day that cracked leg broke in half right as I hit a bank shot off of the corner sending the black 8 ball ricocheting in the pocket where I intended for it to go. As soon as the 8 ball hit the pocket the table came crashing downing to the floor. The flaws in the table had caught up with me and needed to be fixed immediately if I was going to continue to play the game of pool. I tried everything to fix that pool table leg myself. I super glued it, cemented it, gorilla bonded it and even duct taped it. All of those were useless temporary fixes for a problem that exceeded beyond my level of expertise and experience.

I asked my son, who wanted to grow up to be an engineer what he suggested I should do to fix the table. He looked at me and he said "daddy I would suggest that you take the table to someone that knows how to fix pool tables'. Wow, I thought to myself, his answer was so simple but exactly what I needed to do. I needed to take the pool table to someone that knew how to fix it. I called around and finally found someone that could fix the pool table and they fixed it and it's been fine every since and my pool game has greatly increased. The lesson I learned from that experience was that we all have something that is broken in our lives. It could be a broken appliance in our home, a broken vehicle or a broken pool table. It could be a broken relationship with our significant other, our family members or someone in our daily lives.

It could even be a broken relationship with ourselves, a broken promise or a broken dream deferred. We could be the victims of a broken spirit, a broken home or a broken faith. Whatever it is that is broken in our lives that is hindering us from reaching our potential we need to fix it or we need to go to someone that has the knowledge, wisdom and ability to fix it. When I bought that pool table that I described above, it was broke when I got it but I thought I could fix it myself. I fixed it temporarily but it was still broken and eventually the damage that I caused by ignoring the real problem ended up costing me a lot of valuable time, energy and financial resources. If you're going to live up to your potential you're going to need to obtain the tools of knowledge, wisdom and understanding that can fix the broken places in your life.

An Eraser- If you're going to live up to your potential you're going to need a good eraser. In life you're going to make some mistakes. Some mistakes you can erase and move on as if it never happened and some mistakes you can never erase and you must live with the consequences of those mistakes for the rest of your life. When you make mistakes in life which we will all do, the key is to erase away enough of the negative mental residue from that mistake so that it does not hinder you from learning from it and moving forward. It is important that you do not continually beat yourself over the head in disgrace and disappointment when you make a bad decision. If you're anything like me you will need a big eraser to carry around with you in life because sometimes you will make some big mistakes. The single biggest mistake that I've made and continue to make is the mistake of thinking that I know everything. In actuality all I know is what I think I know, and in reality, I don't know anything beyond that which I know. Be it out of ignorance, impatience or inconsideration of the consequences, you will make mistakes in all areas of your life. When you make a mistake in life it doesn't mean that you are a failure, it just means that you are human. The beauty of the eraser is its forgiveness, it gives you the power to erase some of your mistakes, dust yourself off, get up and start over again. A good eraser will help you to keep moving towards your goals and potential.

Rose Colored Glasses- Clear vision and focus is required to navigate successfully to your goals. If you're to get from here to there you need to keep your eyes on the prize. Have you ever got ready to go to a club on a Saturday night? You were looking good, feeling good, smelling good and told yourself you were going to have a good time. You get to the club, you go in and the vibe is right and everything is going great.

The women in the club are looking good, smelling good and sounding good and you tell yourself "I'm going to pull me a dime piece tonight and make her my queen."

As the night goes on you're having yourself a good time. You're enjoying the fun, seductive atmosphere, you're enjoying the company of the lady sitting across from you and you're enjoying the hypnotic rhythmic pulsating beat coming from the powerful 10,000 watt sound systems in the club. At about a quarter to two in the morning the DJ comes over the sound system and he's says "last call for alcohol." What the DJ is saying is; in about 15 minutes the alcohol is going to stop flowing, the music is going to stop playing, the lights are going to be turned on and the rose colored glasses are going to come off and you're going to see the club for what it really is. It's not going to be some high class night club full of beautiful, happy and attentive women.

It's not going to be the seductive lion's den with the red lights that make everybody look good with smooth skin and white teeth. No, No, No my friend. The rose colored glasses are going to come off as soon as they turn on the lights and you're going to see the club for what it really is. A little dirty dingy nightclub on the seedy part of town where everybody in the club is broke, broken, busted and disgusted. Once the rose colored glasses come off and the lights come on, dreams of you making that lady you were talking to all night your beautiful queen are destroyed when you can clearly see that her mustache is thicker than yours and that she is more man than you could ever be.

You desperately need a good pair of rose colored glasses to shield you from the harsh realities of life that can crush your dreams and deter you from reaching your potential. Your rose colored glasses are the belief that you can make it in spite of what you see. Your rose colored glasses is the faith that keeps you focused on the prize, the "dime pieces of Life" and your goals. Without a strong faith to shield you, your vision and potential will perish.

Reliable Transportation- At some point as you're riding down the highway of life on your way to your goals and dreams the road is not always going to be clear. You will have to ride through the rain and the storms and the ride will get downright bumpy. The bumps may cause you to temporarily postpone your journey and delay you from reaching your destination. Reaching your potential sometimes may mean that you have to cut some people loose or you may need to add some people such as good mentors and role models. One of my favorite movies is a movie called Get On The Bus. It's the story of a group of men that get on a bus that is taking them to the million man march. On the way to the march the men run into all kinds of difficulties. The frustrations of the ride causes the men on the bus to start fussing, fighting and complaining.

It got so bad that the driver of the bus literally threw some of the men off the bus and even threw some of the men under the bus but one thing the driver made clear was that the bus was going to keep on moving. Later in their journey the bus finally broke down and left all of the men stranded on a deserted road in the middle of the night. The men realized that they were stuck and the chances of them reaching their intended destination were quickly fading with each hour that slowly passed by.

The men eventually arrived at their intended destination however they arrived too late to realize their goal of attending all of the rallies, marches and hearing a word that they felt would energize and inspire them to change their lives for the better.

I learned a few things from watching that powerful movie. The first thing I learned is that on your road to realizing your potential you must know where you're going, how to get there and you must have the necessary reliable vehicle to get you there. The second thing I learned from watching Get On The Bus is that everybody that is riding with you don't necessarily want to see you arrive at your destination, they are just there to ensure that you don't make it.

The final thing I learned from watching the movie is that you better have a backup plan and options to get you to where you're trying to go. The most powerful part of the movie was at the end. Even though the bus broke down most of the men still got to their destination and there were some men that never made it. Some were kicked off the bus along the way and some literally died on the journey.

Some literally got on the bus in chains and some got off the bus in chains that they placed on themselves. Some never intended to make it to the final destination but by divine fate everyone that was on that bus was on that bus for a reason and everything that they went through served a purpose that was bigger than any one individual. What was so powerful about the end of that movie was that you realized that the ride on that bus was not about the destination it was about the journey.

Each man on that bus experienced life changing events that changed them forever. All of the obstacles and setbacks caused them to come face to face with what their purpose was. When they arrived at their deserted destination

a day late after everything had ended and all of the people had gone home, they realized that it wasn't the rallies, the marches or the speeches that summons them to get on that bus that day. What drove them to get on that bus was their desire to come together in brotherhood, to gain wisdom to improve their lives and their desire to unburden themselves with the literal and self-imposed shackles that kept them from being the men that they really wanted to be.

As the movie credits began to roll and the voice of Ossie Davis is heard narrating a letter that he wrote before he died on his journey, you see the men standing at the Lincoln Memorial, alone in the dark, united in brotherhood, filled with the wisdom that the dark days on that bus had taught them. No chains, no shackles just men standing there in silence, realizing that it wasn't about the destination, it was about the journey.

Videos On Living Up To Your Potential
Pause here and watch at least two video

The Keys To Success –Eric Thomas-   YouTube

Dr. Eric Thomas Phd–Eric Thomas-   YouTube

Do Not Be Out Worked –Eric Thomas-   YouTube

Armed And Dangerous –Les Brown-   YouTube

I'm The One –Les Brown-   YouTube

When Power Meets Potential – TD Jakes-   YouTube

Any Given Sunday Speech – Al Pacino-   YouTube

Book Notes On How You Can Start Living Up To Your Potential

Chapter 7

"Powerful Goal Setting Tips For Fathers and Sons"

Just about everything that you will achieve or accomplish in life you will have had to have made a conscious decision at some point in your thinking to achieve or accomplish that which you have brought into fruition. The quickest way to accomplish anything is to set goals that will continually bring you one step closer to making it a reality. Goal setting is critical to your success and you will need to know how to set goals effectively to achieve maximum results in the shortest amount of time. If you are to become the successful man that you are destined to become it will require that you set ambitious goals and began immediately executing on them. The power of NOW will prove to be your best servant as you go about achieving your goals. In order to increase your chances of realizing your goals it is best if your goals are specific, significant, and stated in the positive. Having a specific goal will help you to focus on doing the things that are closely aligned with what you are trying to accomplish and will help to ensure that you are not doing things just to be doing them but that you are doing the things that will give you the greatest results.

One of the deterrents to goal setting is the fact that most goals are too small. Make sure that your goals are big enough to capture your imagination and inspire you to want to achieve them. If the goals you set won't change your life in some profound way then you probably will not have the motivation to see them through. The risk of not accomplishing a goal that is too small is greater than the risk of not accomplishing a goal that is big. When you set goals you are more likely to see them through if they are created with a positive mindset with a positive outcome.

Many times we set goals as a way to avoid a negative outcome or consequence if we don't accomplish them. This mindset will subconsciously have you focusing on the negative outcomes that could happen instead of focusing on the positive rewards that we are truly seeking. Make sure your goals are about creating something positive, not escaping something negative. One of the key things to remember in goal setting is the fact that unless your goals are written out and reviewed daily then it's not a goal, it's a wish. Goals must be written down and thought about daily. There is a study that states that the average person will only accomplish 20% of their goals. What this means is that when you start goal setting most of your goals will go unrealized because they weren't really goals at all, they were desires.

The process of writing down your goals will help you to clarify exactly what is really worth your time and energy to pursue. Another key thing to remember in goal setting is that your goals must be aligned with what your true values are. Make sure your goals are really yours and not someone else's goals that you feel you should carry out and accomplish. Don't let your parents, friends, or culture dictate your goals. Your goals must be aligned with your core values. Before you began to start executing on a goal remember that every goal has a cost and a price that you will pay to achieve it. Count up the costs involved and decide whether you want to accept this cost. Is the goal worth the cost? The cost of a goal might be time, money, emotional labor, or some other form of sacrifice. Perhaps there is a real tradeoff between accepting the new management position and spending time with your family. Perhaps you have to risk your life savings to start your first business. Perhaps you have to give up your favorite food to drop 50 pounds. Are you willing to accept these costs? If not, you won't succeed.

Don't undertake a new goal lightly, but also don't focus so much on the cost that it scares you from acting. Everything we accomplish in life takes steps. To help us achieve our desires we need to set goals. As a Man your life should be about setting and reaching goals and each time you do this you should set the bar a little higher each time. You should have goals that you want to achieve for yourself, your family, your relationships, your children, your church and your community. As a Man you should always be striving to make life better for you and others. Sometimes setting goals can be overwhelming when you look at all of the little steps that you have to execute on to accomplish them. You should be doing something every day that helps to get you one step closer to your dreams and goals.

Tips That Will Help You To Create And Achieve More In Less Time

Pick One Goal- *This is important! You can only achieve your goals if you focus on them one at a time. Once your goal has been accomplished or made into a stable habit you can start on the next goal. Remember doing things, is not the same as getting things done.*

Start Small and Easy- *The best way to succeed with your first goal is to pick something you are already doing, once in awhile, but want to do daily. This will build your self confidence as you achieve the goal and help prepare you to work on future goals.*

Simplify- *Choose a small, specific goal, or break up larger goals into small pieces that can be done on a daily basis. Big successes start with little ones.*

Write It Down- *Write your goal in large letters and place it where you will see it several times a day. Putting your goal to paper makes it official: You Want It!*

Keep Track Every Day- *This step is very important! If you don't keep track of your daily progress you won't progress. Everything we accomplish takes daily steps, which turns the goal into a habit.*

You Have To Want It- *If you don't really want to do it, you won't succeed. Pick goals you want to achieve or change your attitude so that you really do want it.*

Schedule Time- *Here are some ideas to help you make time for your goal Prioritize: Make time by not doing things that are of less, or no, value. Learn to say No: Learn to gracefully say no to those who ask for your time when you already have too much to do. Saying no can be done in a kind way, just be clear that you cannot do what is being asked of you.*

Make the Time- *You have to make the time or you won't make the goal. Pick a time when you will work on your goal, such as early in the morning, late at night, during lunch, when your children are sleep, watching TV, playing or when you're waiting in line for something. If you don't have the time then wake up earlier. Most people only need 6 hours of deep sleep. If you have trouble sleeping try the following: don't eat after 8:00 and don't rehearse the day's events or tomorrow's plan. Instead focus your mind continually on a black hole of nothing.*

Be Firm Yet Flexible- *To achieve your goal you have to be firm with yourself. You have to do the required work to accomplish your goal. You also have to be flexible. Make a backup plan for days when achieving your goal might be difficult. If your goal is to study the scriptures daily and you know on Friday you'll be running errands the entire day take your scriptures with you. Study them during the moments you're waiting for something to happen, such as standing in line. Be firm with yourself. Also, if your goal is something that you want to do six days a week but not on Sundays you can pick a similar activity to replace your goal. For example: One of my goals is to work on my writing, so on Sundays I wrote a chapter in my book which counts towards achieving my daily goal.*

Be Positive- *Doubting thoughts, and words, will crush your goal. Think and say positive things. If your goal is to eat healthier you could say, "I'm grateful I only eat healthy foods" or if you want to be more patient say, "I'm thankful I'm patient." it really works. It has turned my most negative, consistent thoughts into a positive reality.*

Pray About It- *Choosing righteous goals is just what the Lord wants us to do, so ask for his help. As you pray daily and work towards your goal you will see daily success. I can't begin to tell you how I accomplished some of the things I have other than to tell you that it was the only by the grace of God and the favor he has shown me. Most of the times when I accomplished anything of significance all I had to do was to walk into it as the provisions had already been made for me to succeed. I was equipped and prepared to see my goal come into fruition. Prayer is one of your super weapons.*

An Effective 30 day Goal Setting Journal That Will Help You To Accomplish More In Less Time

Write down three things that you are grateful for every day

Write down three goals that you want to accomplish in the next 30 days and write these down everyday

Write down three things that you will do today that will get you one step closer to your goal. Write these down everyday

Write down three things that you will do today to improve your health and physical well being. Write these down everyday

Write down three positive things that you noticed today. Write these down everyday

Write down what you will do to celebrate achieving the goals that you wrote down. Write this down every day.

Videos On Goal Setting
Pause here and watch at least one video on Youtube

Goal Setting –Zig Ziglar -

How To Reach Your Goals And Dreams –Les Brown -

5 Common Myths About Goal Setting –Brian Tracy -

How To Follow Through –Tony Robbins -

Chapter 8

"Teach Him How To Make His Own Money"

In your journey as a man how you earn your money is just as important as how much money you are able to earn. The money that you earn and more importantly how you earn it, will provide you with the opportunities to live the type of lifestyle that you've always dreamed of and provide for the people and causes that mean the most to you. Your ability to help other people, organizations and causes that you believe it will be greatly increase in direct proportion to your willingness and desire to develop the necessary skills, talents and creativity to earn more money through multiple streams of income.

This chapter will provide you with some principles regarding money and a guide to help young men and single mothers start small businesses that will start you out on your path to entrepreneurship and being able to provide financially for you and your family. The business opportunities in this chapter deals primarily with businesses that just about anyone can start and these business opportunities can be used as an additional stream of income for the person that is already established in his or her career and looking for some quick and simple side business ideas. Are you the type of person that has been thinking about starting a business, but you've been procrastinating, waiting for just the right time?

Do you think conditions have to be just right before you can move forward? Are you wondering when, exactly, is the best time to launch your business idea? You will know when the time is right when the following events occur:

The economy is hot. In a booming economy potential clients have more money, and you probably have more money to invest in your business. It's the best time to be optimistic.

The economy is cold. Bad economies often lead to creative solutions and ideas. Many a millionaire has been created during a down economy.

You've lost your job or sense downsizing. Other sources of income are necessary.

Your skills are in great demand. Supply and demand brings new opportunities.

You're going through life changes. Sometimes the best time to start something new is when the old is fading away.

You can't take it anymore. You have a burning desire to try something new and different.
If you haven't figured it out yet, NOW is the best time to start the exciting journey and challenges of starting your own business and start making money NOW.

This Sixth law of Make More Money Have More Fun is a guide of tips, tools and business startup ideas that you can use to start making money Right Now. The money principles and business ideas in this guide are tried, true, proven and have the ability to improve your life and those around you. All of the business ideas contained within this guide can be started with little to no capital investment and your business can be up and running and making money within 30 days or less. There are countless ways in today's economy to create, earn and generate an extra source of income. You may be looking for an idea to make some extra pocket change, spending money for entertainment expenses, gas or to pay a cable bill.

You may be looking for ways to supplement your current income, pay a car note or mortgage payment each month or any myriad of expenses that come with life. In this short easy to read guide to starting a business you will find 5 different in demand opportunities that will address many of your financial needs, satisfy the entrepreneurial spirit within and provide you with a life changing opportunity that you can share with others. More than ever there is a need to seize opportunities that will provide us with the financial security and self-improvement that we need to survive in today's economic climate. Yet there seems to be a reluctance to take the necessary risks and steps that are required to maintain or reach beyond our current standard of living. I believe this cautiousness results not from a lack of competence, ambition or drive but from a lack of knowledge in regards to proven, legitimate business opportunities that will generate an income that will make the journey, capital and physical investment worthwhile. Within the pages of this guide hopefully you will find something that will spark an interest, drive you to action or at the very least stir up the creative juices that have lain dormant in the corridors of your mind.

This is not a get rich quick scheme, a magic spell that cures all or even a promise of success but if you sincerely desire the spark to get you heading in the right entrepreneurial spirit then this guide will be a fitting catalyst. This guide does not provide a comprehensive insight into any potential losses, failures, risks, tax implications, liabilities or legal requirements to operate each business. This guide is a beneficial outline of how to start each business and the steps that will help you start earning money immediately. Some of the businesses listed may or may not appeal to you however you can substitute whatever product or service you wish to provide and use the same concepts that you will find here.

5 Businesses You Can Start Right Now

These Businesses are perfect for the young man or single mother looking to make extra income to support his or her family

Business #1- Personal Life Coach

Business #2- Creative Merchandising Business

Business #3- Full Service Wedding Provider

Business #4- Internet Flipping and Buying

Business #5- Video Production Business

Business 1- Personal Life Coach

The path to becoming a personal development consultant begins with you. While formal training is ideal, education, a social network and experience developing yourself are essential first steps. A personal development consultant examines the fiscal, physical, mental and spiritual/moral components of a client's life and assesses how to build and maximize on those personal assets to achieve the desired success. You can use your own experiences, professional and personal successes to build your reputation and attract clients. There is an unlimited market of people that are looking for personal and professional guidance from a competent consultant with a listening ear that can help them refocus or redirect their path in life. You as a skilled Personal Development Consultant can fill that void. The top specialty areas that attracts the most clients are:

Financial Advice – financial basics that include how to budget and live within your means, how to improve your credit score, how the stock market and investments work, how to start a small business, facilitate financial seminars, resume building, job interview preparation, financial basics for kids

Relationship Counseling- relationship advice, how to attract the right people into your life, overcoming setbacks in a relationship, match making, how to gain and maintain respect in your relationship, how to become more desirable to the opposite sex, why men cheat, why women cheat, the 3 types of men that women love and hate at the same time, the 3 type of women that men should avoid but don't, being honest with yourself and having the relationship you deserve

Attitude Improvement- how to develop a positive mental and physical attitude regardless of the circumstances, how to deal with negative people, the law of attraction, the law of sowing and reaping, developing self worth and improving your self esteem, how astrology affects your attitude and how to use it to your advantage, finding opportunities all around you daily

Finding Passion and Purpose – finding your purpose, what are you really good at, determining what you really want in life, what makes you tick and get you motivated, always having something to look forward to, determining who or what needs you the most, leaving a legacy

Writing and Selling How To Books – If you have an expertise in a given area that is in high demand, put your ideas in a short how to book. Getting your book published is relatively inexpensive these days. You can write a book and publish it with major online outlets such as Amazon, Barnes and Noble and Kindle.

Personal Life Coach

Qualities required to become a Personal Development Consultant

Good listening skills

Communication skills,

Rapport-building,

Motivating and Inspiring,

Applicable life experiences

Desire and Courage to help others improve

How to start your business as a Personal Development Consultant

1.) Determine your specialty areas of interest
2.) Attend free life coaching seminars or study courses online
3.) Network with other seasoned personal development consultants

4.) Identify potential clients to work with for free to gain experience
5.) Create business cards and flyers to distribute at events, job fairs, etc.
6.) Find a secure location to meet clients, home, parks, church, hotel lobbies
7.) Provide initial 15 minute consultation to determine clients needs
8.) Provide client with confidentiality and service contracts
9.) Maintain records of progress and success until desire result is achieved

How to find clients and generate money

1.) Network at business events, expos, chamber of commerce, conferences
2.) Church, Civic, fraternal, sorority organizations,
3.) Word of mouth, salons, spas, gyms
4.) Conduct seminars on hot topics and charge a nominal entrance fee
5.) Receive referral fees from seasoned consultants
6.) Job placement offices, unemployment security commission, shelters
7.) Establish an online presence, create website, media press release, news ads

Business 2- Creative Merchandising may be calling you if you enjoy creating your own unique line of merchandise, designing and selling your own private label clothing. If opening up your own store is your dream, please keep the following in mind. Starting your own boutique or retail store require many skills, significant time investment and a huge outlay of cash just to get your doors open and ready for opening day. Those who enter the business should also have retail experience, know fashion trends, and specialize in a particular market. Administrative cost, advertising, shipping cost, Business travel, market research, building lease, operating equipment, inventory, payroll, legal fees, utilities, taxes, insurance and a host of other expenses can drive your initial startup cost from $150,000 to $300,000 just to get into the business and those cost still do not guarantee you success.

If you happen to be one of the fortunate entrepreneurs that have a solid business plan, a cadre of designers and distributors foaming at the mouth to serve you, a great building location with lots of foot traffic and $150,000 - $300,000 to start your business, congratulations are in order!! If you have a lot of drive, ambition, creativity and desire but very little cash, do not despair.

There is a way to realize your dreams of starting your own line of unique merchandise and have them displayed and selling in high traffic, upscale, established boutiques for a fraction of the cost, headaches and time investment it normally requires.

How to start your Unique Merchandising Business

1.) Decide what type of merchandise you wish to create and sell
2.) Research the market, your target demographics, trends and conduct surveys
3.) Design, create and obtain temporary trademark for your initial product and logo
4.) Secure reputable product distributor for a small initial inventory, set cost points
5.) Locate, establish rapport with local boutique owners that match your target market
6.) Present your product and solicit a consignment agreement
7.) Negotiate shelf space, consignment agreement, inventory and marketing
8.) Establish an online presence, eBay, etsy, yak, create website, affiliate marketing

Tips to negotiating fees, costs, shelf space, terms, increasing sales and visibility

1.) Attend networking expos, conferences, chamber of commerce, street vendors
2.) Use distributors of other vendors to save on costs of initial inventory
3.) Offer free advertising in exchange for shelf space and waiver of consignment fees
4.) Negotiate shelf or table space in advance at events that require vendors fees
5.) Have family, friends, students, church, civic organizations pass out ad flyers

Business 3- Wedding Consulting is a very good way to earn extra income. According to industry statistics there are approximately 2.5 million weddings performed in the U.S. each year and the wedding industry generates over $40 billion dollars per year. Several sectors of our society are affected or influenced in some way by the joining of two people in the bonds of matrimony. The wedding process generates revenues for many corporations and industries. This includes clothing, flowers, food, transportation, lodging, music, legal, religion, travel and a host of other goods and services. The wedding ceremony in and of itself runs on average anywhere from $2,600.00 to $25,000 with some ceremonies costing upwards of $1 million dollars. There is an unlimited market of clients that cannot afford and even more that choose not to pay the astronomical cost associated with having a traditional wedding. The need for a more economical and professional alternative is in high demand. This is where you

as a Full Service Wedding Provider can fill that void. With the right skills, creativity, and knowledge you will be well on your way to creating a fun, exciting, and money making business. Within 30 days you can be enjoying the financial, social and recession proof benefits that comes with being a part of a couple's most special day. If you follow this guide you will be well on your way to tapping into a $40 billion dollar industry and carving out your small but extremely profitable niche of the matrimonial pie. You can now acquire the power, authority and expertise to become a licensed wedding professional and have the ability to offer the following affordable wedding ceremonies and more. Non-Denominational Chapel Ceremony, Horse and Carriage Ceremony Beautiful Outdoor Garden Ceremony, Evening Candlelight Ceremony, Beach Front Ceremony
Down town Rooftop Skyline Ceremony.

How to start a Full Service Wedding Provider Business

1.) *Become a licensed wedding officiant*
2.) *Obtain a wedding guide checklist and a ceremony procedure guide*
3.) *Obtain business cards, flyers and business cell phone message*
4.) *Contact local wedding planners and offer service for minimal fee to gain experience*
5.) *Create an online presence and build provider contact lists*

Tips to minimize costs, attract clients and expand your business

1.) *Provide pre-recorded music, photography and keepsake certificate*
2.) *If you have a nice luxury car provide transportation, champagne toast*
3.) *Choose sites with natural scenery, flowers and ambience*
4.) *Target clients at the court house, county clerk's office and hang up flyers*

Business 4- Internet Buying and Flipping

Flipping is buying or obtaining merchandise at very little cost and selling it quickly for a profit. There are several shows on TV such as Storage Wars, Flip this house *Flip This House, Pawn Stars and Property*

100

Ladder that has increased the popularity of flipping. You can flip just about anything. Cars, homes, artwork, vintage toys, antiques, furniture, bicycles, motorcycles, jewelry and the list is endless. This is a very fun and profitable business if you obtain the right merchandise to flip. I've bought and flipped watches, video equipment, motorcycles and cars. I started a flip with an expensive watch which I ended up trading for a motorcycle. I traded that motorcycle for a classic sports car for which I was offered two more cars in exchange for the one sports car. I will more than likely be trading the sports car to pay for my son's college education at the university which includes a year's worth of tuition, books, room and board. Not a bad flip that started with a watch.

How to start your Internet Buying and Flipping Business

1.) Find merchandise in your home that you no longer want that has value
2.) Visit yard sales, thrift stores, attic sales, flea markets and find merchandise
3.) Negotiate the lowest possible purchasing price for merchandise
4.) Clean up or repair merchandise if needed and take good pictures
5.) Find items online such as craigslist, Ebay and Angie's list
6.) Use creative free marketing and ad presentation services
7.) Create an online presence and list merchandise with a profitable margin

Merchandise that make for profitable buying and flipping

1.) Vintage toys from the 60's, 70's and 80's
2.) Classic men's watches
3.) Slightly used new looking furniture
4.) Electronics, cameras and used cell phones that are high demand
5.) Oil painting reproductions of famous artists such as Rembrandt, Picasso, Van Gogh
6.) Designer brand named clothing such as Polo, Neiman, Zelda, Brooks Brothers
7.) Classic inexpensive sports cars from the 80's that need do it yourself repairs

Business 5- Photography & Video Production Business

Instagram, Facebook , Modeling, Selfies, YouTube and self-branding have all made photography and videography an interesting way to earn additional income and have fun doing it. If you know your way around a camera, a camcorder and editing software then starting your own photography and video production business is a way to make some quick fun money. In addition to flexible working hours and diversity of clients and assignments, photography and video production is a business you can launch with a relatively small amount of capital as well as promote very easily via the internet and customer referrals. Creating quality YouTube channels and programming is hugely popular. Photos are extremely popular these days and having a professional camera or camcorder in your hand is a good way to meet new people and make money at the same time.

How to start your Video Production Business

1.) Purchase a digital video camcorder and digital camera
2.) Obtain use of computer with editing software and dvd burner loaded onto it
3.) Attend free events, shoot video and take pictures to gain experience
4.) Download film footage to editing software and practice burning dvds
5.) Obtain business cards, flyers and pass out at events

Tips to minimize costs, attract clients and expand your business

1.) Purchase used equipment online, pawn shops, yard sales and flea markets
2.) Network at video production events, weddings, family reunions, sporting events e
3.) Obtain an online presence, website and affiliate marketing
4.) Offer to produce documentaries on little known but talented people in your city
5.) Advertise to provide your services at reunions, CIAA tournament, churches and school

Spiritual Thoughts & Scriptures on Money

For the men that are looking for spiritual financial guidance or are curious about God's thoughts concerning your money, I believe that the following spiritual money principles will aid you in making wise decisions concerning your money. If you've asked yourself the question what is God's thought about your money, God has a lot to say about your money. Not only does he have a plan for you, but He also has principles and a purpose for your money. Let's look at some of God's thought's concerning your money. Share this with your sons.

Share and give it

But do not forget to do good and to share, for with such sacrifices God is well pleased. Hebrews 13:16

God wants you to be a giver. He wants you to increase so you can be a blessing and help others better themselves. What's the point in getting rich if it's only for you? So what, you've now got a really nice house and car...and then what? Of course you can do what you want with the money you earned, but in God's system there's far more to be gained from giving to others. Actually this is a very important principle that you need to know; God *"...supplies seed to the sower" 2 Corinthians 9:10*. If you're not sowing than why should God keep supplying you with seed?

Help others less fortunate

If a brother or sister is naked and destitute of daily food, 16 and one of you says to them, "Depart in peace, be warmed and filled," but you do not give them the things which are needed for the body, what does it profit? James 2:15-16

There will be times when we can and should help those who are less fortunate by giving what we have. This is true love. God actually says that we are lending to Him. *He who has pity on the poor lends to the Lord. And He will pay back what he has given. Proverbs 19:17*

Be wise with your money

For even when we were with you, we commanded you this: If anyone will not work, neither shall he eat. 2 Thessalonians 3:10

It's easy to say give to those in need. But there is also a time to hold back on your giving. Sometimes we must seriously check whether, in our attempts to help, we are really being a blessing. If someone refused to work or get a job and you kept giving them money and they spent it on going out and having fun then you're probably creating a bigger problem then you realize.

Work for it

In all labour there is profit, but idle chatter leads only to poverty. Proverbs 14:23

If you're waiting for the lottery to make you rich so you don't have to work another day then you're missing the point. It's in our work that we discover what we value, what gifts we have and how far our ability can stretch. Even if you're in a job that you don't like that should be provoking you to discover what else you could do.

Manage it well

His lord said to him, 'Well done, good and faithful servant; you were faithful over a few things, I will make you ruler over many things. Enter into the joy of your lord.' Matthew 25:21

Of course God wants to increase you. But what if He kept giving you money and you kept squandering it? Does that make you a faithful steward that God should continue to increase? You need to learn to be faithful with even the little you have received. God respects that.

Increase and multiply it

Then God blessed them, and God said to them, 'Be fruitful and multiply; fill the earth and subdue it...' Genesis 1:28

God's mandate to mankind was our increase. We are suppose to increase in that which is fruitful and good and decrease in that which causes pain and goes against God's laws.

When you really begin to love God's wisdom, He will cause you to inherit wealth *I traverse the way of righteousness, In the midst of the paths of justice, That I may cause those who love me to inherit wealth, That I may fill their treasuries. Proverbs 8:20-21*

That doesn't just mean being a person of prayer and good morals, but rather it means also respecting God's principles concerning wealth and life.

Set a foundation for future generations

'A good man leaves an inheritance to his children's children...' Proverbs 13:22

All of us were not born into a nice inheritance with some good financial teaching to go with it, however, there's nothing stopping you from setting up future generations with that which you didn't have. That's why you have to succeed in life; so you can leave some kind of legacy of wealth and wisdom for future generations.

Build His kingdom on earth

And you shall remember the LORD your God, for it is He who gives you power to get wealth that He may establish His covenant which He swore to your fathers, as it is this day. Deuteronomy 8:18

God's plan stretched from the present until eternity. His desire is that no soul on this earth should perish, but that all will come to know His saving love and grace through Jesus Christ. *2 Peter 3:9* God wants to bless so we can be a blessing in our deeds, love and actions. There are really special prizes in eternity for those that can win souls.

Enjoy it!

Command those who are rich in this present age not to be haughty, nor to trust in uncertain riches but in the living God, who gives us richly all things to enjoy. 1Timothy 6:17

Keep your trust in God and continually build a relationship with Him, but while you're doing that enjoy what He gives you. Be wise, but every now and again treat yourself with something nice. Because, contrary to some beliefs... ***You're Worth It!***

Videos On Business And Money
Pause here and watch at least one video below

7 Baby Steps —Dave Ramsey-
YouTube

5 Things For Financial Success—Dave Ramsey-
YouTube

Don't Go Into Debt To Buy Stupid Stuff—Dave Ramsey-
YouTube

How To Start A Business In 2015 With No Money —Glendon Cameron-
YouTube

Chapter 9

"Perception And Reality Are Extremely Important"

When a man first steps into a room, he does not have to say a word, his appearance, his confidence and his nonverbal communication will speak volumes. How you present yourself matters in a real way that will affect a man's daily life from how you are greeted when meeting others for the first time to whether or not you'll be harassed while walking down the street or entering public establishments. How you dress and how you carry yourself as a man goes a long way in creating a positive first impression.

You will find that people can be drawn to the superficial at times and tend to make snap judgments based on what they see when they first meet you. Their initial opinions of you have already been formed before they've actually spoken to you or had a chance to get to know what you are all about. This means that how you present yourself and how you dress are going to have a direct effect on people's assumptions of you.

Generally the better you're dressed, the more respect and attention people are going to automatically give you. The way you dress and carry yourself can increase your perceived status among your peers and the people that you come in contact with. Even after the first impression is over, the way you dress and carry yourself can aid in improving people's perception of you and reactions to you. Society is very visually-based and better-dressed men routinely experience better treatment and service than their less well put together counterparts. The way you dress and carry yourself serves as a representation in the eyes of people who don't know you of who they think you are. This will be the primary factor by which you're judged when they don't know enough to judge you by anything else.

The way you dress and your outer appearance may sound superficial, but it should never be taken for granted as it serves as an advertisement for your own personal branding. Your dress and your personal branding will help you to stand out as a man and differentiate you from being the average male and present you as a man of value and a man that knows where he's going. If you are the type of man where your appearance may not mean that much to *you*, please know that your appearance means a lot to the people that you come in contact with every day. When you walk into a room your appearance will have a direct affect on how the people in the room feel about you and the energy that you bring into that encounter. How you present yourself and how you are dress will either enhance or erode their impression of you and how they feel about what you represent at that particular moment. There are many benefits to dressing well other than the positive reactions of those that you meet. Carrying yourself in a certain manner and dressing well will dramatically increase your self-confidence.

As we discussed in the previous chapters, self- confidence is one the main characteristic that you must possess as a man if you look to obtain any level of success in any area of your life. One of the first pieces of advice you will often hear people say when you are looking to improve yourself is the advice to upgrade your personal appearance as it is the easiest upgrade you can make and it has an immediate and powerful impact on your personal branding and confidence level.

When your personal appearance has been upgraded you will tend to feel better, perform better and subconsciously you will feel like you *deserve* better. The automatic assumption that a well-dressed man will be treated with a little more respect than a lesser dresser man tends to be true in most cases where people tend to judge you on your outer appearance more so that who you are on the inside. When you spend a few more minutes putting yourself together and a little more care in how you present yourself you will find that the dividends it pays is well worth the investment.

As a man one of the best ways to articulate your skills, experience, knowledge, and overall worth is to create a personal brand that helps you stand out in the crowd. If you wish to speak volumes without saying a word you will need to become the marketing director of Me Inc. As the marketing director of Me Inc. your most important job is to be head marketer of a brand called You. The uniqueness of you should draw people to your product, services or your message. Personal branding is really about who you are and what you have to offer. One thing I know from personal experience is that if you don't develop your own personal brand others will develop it for you.

Personal branding is a proactive way of controlling how you are perceived by others as well as a way to take control of your personal and career development. The following tips will help you to become successful in your role as your own marketing director and it will assist and guide you in developing a powerful personal brand.

Tips to Developing a Powerful Personal Brand

Determine your unique value - *Determine what makes you different than your peers. What are your strengths, your passions and your goals? Ask yourself the question, if I left my job or position today, what would my company or colleagues miss the most about me? Be sure to know who you are, as well as who you are not and what you bring to the table.*

Find out how others see you- *Be willing to ask people that you trust, co-workers, and friends for four or five adjectives that truthfully and accurately describe you. Have them tell you what they think you are good at, what are your strengths and in what areas do they view you as being irreplaceable.*

Identify What Your Goals Are- *Where do you want to be in 6 months, a year or 5 years from now? Knowing what your goals are and being able to define and articulate them will help you in creating a personal branding message that will help you reach them.*

Be Clear On Who Your Target Audience Is- *You need to identify who your target audience is for your branding message and why you chose that particular audience.*

Knowing this will help you to create the right message for the audience that you are trying to reach.

Re-organize Your Priorities- *You will need to become somewhat selfish when it comes to developing your personal brand. This is all about you and you must be comfortable being loyal to yourself and the brand that you have created for yourself.*

Pay Attention To The Details- *Realize that everything that you do, every day, contributes to your personal brand. Once you have defined your brand make sure that the little things including the way you dress, your body language, how you behave, what you say and don't say, your communication are all consistent with your brand message.*

Update Your Resume- *Review your resume to determine if it is consistent with your brand. Your resume must accurately defines who you are, and is in line with both your short-term and long-term goals.*

Become Active On Social Networks- *You must establish a presence on social networking sites such as Facebook, Twitter and relevant Blogs. Get those in your target audience to subscribe to your pages, and update your communications on these sites on a daily basis. Make sure your updates are pertinent to your branding message.*

Develop Your Own Website- *Your personal website should highlight your professional accomplishments, your skills and knowledge, what you stand for, and your overall value. Make it primarily about you, not your company or clients.*

Create Your Own Blog- *Blogging make it is easier than ever to promote yourself to your target audience. Commit to posting a couple of times a week on topics that your audience will find interesting and educational, but that also highlight your unique skills and experience.*

Write A Book That Gets Published-*Write a book using your experiences and knowledge in your area of expertise, contribute to industry publications, consistently update contents on your website. Being published is an ideal way to promote yourself as an expert in your field.*

Promote Yourself In Person-*Be sure to promote your brand in person as often as possible. Join and participate in industry groups, give talks at conferences, or offer to spearhead a large project that highlights your unique talents.*

Tend To Your Marketing Network-_Be sure to keep co-workers, colleagues, clients, and friends updated about what you are doing. Word of mouth is a powerful marketing tool, and what the people in your network say about you will ultimately have an effect on your brand._

Review Your Brand Frequently- _Always portray your brand in a way that's concise and easily understood. Make sure that your brand's message is consistent among all platforms. A regular review of your brand will ensure your message remains clear._

Sell Yourself On The Idea Of Personal Branding-_You must sell yourself on the idea of branding If you want to be successful. Creating a personal brand isn't just an option, it's a necessity. Whether you aspire to get that promotion or land your dream job, creating a compelling and consistent brand will help you meet your goals._

Videos On Personal Branding And Dress For Success
Please pause and watch at least one video

Dress For Success For Less   –Men's Warehouse-
YouTube Video

How To Dress Well For Men
YouTube Video

Personal Branding Education
YouTube Video

Personal Branding Four Principles Of Career Distinction
YouTube Video

Chapter 10

"Being A Leader Is Not An Option, It is Mandatory"

Out of all of the responsibilities and roles that we as men can hold, none is more important and impactful than our role as a leader. Behind every successful relationship, family, business, community or nation there is a successful and effective leader. Since the beginning of time, leadership has been a man's birthright and a mantle that we must carry with us at all times. As a man, effective leadership is not an option, it is mandatory. If we are going to fulfill our mission in life we as men must become comfortable in our role as a leader. The unwillingness to assume your role as a leader can have a dramatic effect on your life as well as the lives of those around you.

When I thought about some of things that I wanted to teach my son, teaching him to be a leader in all aspects of his life was at the top of the list. The best place to start in this discussion on leadership is to first answer the question, what is a leader? The standard definition of a leader is: *a person that has the ability to influence the thoughts, attitudes, and behaviors of other in a positive or negative way.* The next question is, what does a leader do? Simply put, a leader leads. A leader gives direction to others and they lead you to a specific goal or destination. One of the prerequisites for leadership for a man is that he must be able to lead himself first and know where he is going.

My first personal experience with becoming a leader was when I was in the fourth grade. We had our annual elementary school PTO night which was our parent teacher organization night. The PTO night was a night where you're parents came to your school and met all of your teachers and the students would perform a musical selection and dance that we learned in our music class. For my class we had to perform a song and line dance called heel

toe. The song was simple, we just sung the words heel toe, heel toe, slide slide slide step. We would sing this little song for about four rounds. My first moment of leadership came when the day before the program my music teacher told me that I would be leading the line dance portion of the performance. My job was to show the parents how the line dance would go and then my class would come in after I started to join in on the dance.

When I was told that I would be leading the dance, at first I was nervous because I was somewhat shy, but after I got started I realized that being a leader kind of felt natural to me. I enjoyed the moment and the attention that I received and it taught me a valuable lesson about accepting the challenges and opportunities that come with being a leader.

 The first thing I learned about leadership is that you have to have a desire to lead. I ended up leading that dance not because I was the best dancer in my class or possessed some extra special talent, not at all considering I had two left feet. I ended up leading that dance because the opportunity presented itself and I chose to lead because something deep down inside of me made me feel like that I must lead it. I found out what that something was later on in life. Another important thing I found out about leadership during that dance program is that everybody is not always going to like you when you take the initiative to lead. When I was chosen to lead that simple dance step some of the other students in the class quickly pointed out that I was not the best dancer, that I wasn't loud enough, that I wasn't this or that. At first that caught me by surprise because I thought that they would be glad that I was leading so that they wouldn't have to. That particular lesson that I learned about leading is a truth that remained true throughout every leadership position that I have ever held.

People love and people hate leaders. It doesn't matter what you are leading there will be opposition and there will be those who aren't happy that you chose to lead. The reasoning for the hate and challenges to your leadership is varied and will not disappear. It comes with the territory of leadership so be sure to develop thick skin, stay focused on your reasons for wanting to lead and always remember your purpose for leading. So that there is no

confusion please understand that there is a difference between being a leader and being in a leadership position. You do not have to have an official position or title to be a leader. You just must have the willingness and ability to influence the direction, behavior and attitudes of others. There are plenty of people in leadership positions that simple are not leading. How do you know that they aren't leading? You know that they aren't leading because they are not leading you anywhere or to any particular goal or vision. As a man you must be leading yourself first to a particular goal or destination and then you must be willing and able to lead others.

Your role as a leader is a gift. It is a gift of self- discovery, a gift of self-development and a gift of knowing that no matter what position or title you may hold, you have the power to make a difference in whatever situation you find yourself in. All you have to do is choose to make a difference and lead. It doesn't matter if you are in elementary school, college, at home, at work or in your community, you can and must be a leader at all times. Being a leader does not mean that you don't listen to the advice, guidance and authority of others, it just means that at any given moment when needed, you are able to impact the behavior and direction of an organization or situation for benefit of the whole.

Tips For The Young Male To Become A Leader

How To Become A leader In Your Home- *As a young man there are several ways that you can become a leader in your home. The first thing you can do is to become an example for your siblings to follow in your home. You should always be mindful of the words that come out of your mouth and the behavior that you exhibit. Whenever you see something that needs to be done in your home such as the garbage needs taken out, a room needs cleaning, the grass needs to be cut, automatically volunteer to take care of these things. If you are not capable of handling what needs to be done make your parents aware that it needs to be done and assist in whatever manner that you can. Another way that you can become a leader in your home is to come up with ways to help save money on household expenses. Turn off lights that are not in use, don't run unnecessary water when taking a shower or brushing your teeth, start a little side business to earn money to help pay for your clothes or extracurricular activity expense.*

How To Become A leader In Your School-*There are several ways to become a leader in your school. You can run for class president or vice president, become a part of the student council, and become an officer in one of your school's*

clubs or organizations. Strive to be the captain on one of your school's sports team. Speak up when you see other students being mistreated. Volunteer for school projects and committees.

How To Become A leader In Your Church- *Your church, Mosque or House of worship can and will play a significant role in preparing you as a young male for leadership. Take advantage of every opportunity to develop your communication and leadership skills by volunteering with the youth missionary groups, community service outreach programs, church plays and productions, music department or just simply express your interest in being groomed for leadership in your church. It does not matter what your age is, you can always find leadership opportunities in your local church. If you can't find one, create one.*

How To Become A leader Of Yourself-*The first person you should be successful at leading is yourself. You should take an honest inventory of your strengths and weaknesses and start working on developing your strengths and working on strengthening your weaknesses. There are a few ways you can start leading yourself. You can start leading yourself by becoming a good follower of a mentor that can teach you how to lead. The second way you can start leading yourself is to start carrying yourself with a higher standard and expectations of yourself. The third way you can start leading yourself is by setting individual goals for yourself and then accomplish them. Each goal that you set you should be setting the bar higher and higher each time. The final way that you can start leading yourself is to develop a high level of discipline in everything that you do. Discipline yourself to eat right, discipline yourself to exercise and stay in peak physical conditioning and discipline yourself to do the things that you have to do to better yourself and others.*

Tips That Will Help You To Become An Effective Leader As A Man

You Must First Be Able To Lead Yourself- *The first person you must be able to lead if you're going to be a leader is yourself. You should take the opportunity to do an honest self-assessment of your skills, talents, strengths and weakness prior to leading. The areas that you need to strengthen you must be willing to get the necessary training and development so that those areas will not affect your ability to lead. In order to lead you must be the type of person that people want to follow.*

You must be willing to see and confront the pink elephant in the room- *If you are going to be a leader you must have your eyes wide open and have the courage to bring awareness to any issues, obstacles or challenges that are detrimental to the success of those that you leading . You must be willing to acknowledge, adapt and respond to any situation you find yourself in and you must convince your team or organization the important of doing so. A leader must never be afraid of the truth.*

You must be willing to make the tough decisions- *As a leader, others are looking to you to be make the tough decisions when needed. People will stand back and watch how you handle difficult decisions and they will either gain or lose respect for you in the process.*

You must believe in your mission-*Leadership is about leading people to a destination or to the culmination of a vision. If you are to get there you must have a total commitment and belief in your mission.*

You Must Be Willing To Sacrifice And Give Of Your Time And Energy. *Hard work and sacrifice is required if you want to be successful. However hard work and sacrifice does not always lead to success. Your creative ideas, intelligence, and innovation can lead you to advancement opportunities.*

Step Out Of The Box And Out Of Your Comfort Zone. *Part of being a leader is your ability to learn and to do new and different things. You must be willing to stand up, step out and stand out to set yourself apart.*

Be Willing To Listen. *Sometimes as a leader it's best to sit back, listen and observe. If you can observe and listen then you may find a lot of the answers you seek right in front you.*

Realize That Your Leadership Position Must Be Used To Benefit Others. *The effectiveness of your leadership is measured by the positive impact that your leadership leaves on those that you serve and serve with and how your leadership benefits others and help the group as a whole realize the goals set before them.*

Videos On Leadership
Pause here and watch at least one video

Developing The leader Within You– John Maxwell-
YouTube Video

5 levels Of Leadership- John Maxwell
YouTube Video

Secret Agents Of Change – TD Jakes
YouTube Video

Leadership Must Listen –TD Jakes
YouTube Video

Book Notes On Things You Can Do To Become A Better Leader

Chapter 11

"Laws Of The Universe That He Must Understand"

Along with a healthy spiritual life and a love for the creator there are some universal and natural laws that if practiced you will find that you will be more content and satisfied in your mission as a man.

\

THE LAW OF BALANCE

You must Practice moderation in all levels of your mind, body, being, and emotions. Pay attention to doing too much or too little in areas of eating, drinking, exercise, work, or communication. The Law of Balance assures us that those who give freely, in the spirit of love and generosity, receive in abundance.

THE LAW OF PROCESS

Take life step by step. Enthusiasm sets the pace, but persistence reaches the goal.

THE LAW OF CHOICES

Destiny is determined by the actions you take as a man. No matter what life dishes out, you choose how you will respond internally. Live each day by choice to do the right thing to the fullest extent. Sometimes choice means giving up something you want for something else you want more.

THE LAW OF PRESENCE

The past is vanished, except in your mind. What is to come is only a dream. We have only this moment. Past and future are bad habits of the mind. Presence lightens the mind, liberates you from anxiety, since only the here and now is real.

THE LAW OF COMPASSION

Compassion is the recognition that we are each doing the best we can within the limits of our current beliefs and capacities. In the natural world you have no friends, you have no enemies; you have only teachers. Let compassion wash away negative thoughts in a wave of love and understanding. We are all joined in this mystery of life.

THE LAW OF FAITH

A higher intelligence is working through all of us for the higher good. There is a purpose for every pleasure and hardship. Listen to the intuitive wisdom of your heart. Faith involves the willingness to stretch yourself, make mistakes and learn from them, and to trust in the process of your life.

THE LAW OF EXPECTATION

In your daily life, if you create positive images, happy circumstances, and successful outcomes, these become real. You have the inherent power to shape your life through the images and expectations you create. Since energy follows thought, we move toward what we can imagine.

THE LAW OF ACTION

Only actually doing brings potential to life. It takes doing to understand and wisdom grows out of practice.

THE LAW OF INTEGRITY

To live in line with your highest vision despite impulses to the contrary. It is intelligent to follow the accepted conventions of your society. Live according to your highest light and more light will be given. Be who you are meant to be.

THE LAW OF CYCLES

Old habits can be changed. The momentum of change ultimately leads us toward greater awareness, wisdom and peace. Embrace both good fortune and adversity for their gifts. Move through the cycles of life without haste or resistance.

THE LAW OF SURRENDER

Embracing a higher will expressed as the wisdom of the heart. Ask, in any situation "What is for the highest good of all concerned?" Have a willingness to welcome each moment without judgment or expectation rather than waste energy struggling against whatever happens.

THE LAW OF UNITY

Leave behind the baggage of fear, envy, conflict, and resentment—fly on wings of understanding and compassion. Begin to see friends and adversaries, loved ones and strangers, through the truth that we are all One Being.

Videos On The Universal Laws
Pause here and watch at least one video

The Secret Universal Laws – Napoleon Hill-
YouTube Video

The Laws Of Attraction – Infinite Waters
YouTube Video

Power Of Mind Power Of Thought –Djehuty Ma'atra
YouTube Video

Motivated And Driven –Daniel Collier
YouTube Video

Chapter 12

"How Not To Be Selfish, Leaving a Legacy"

When I first began to write this book for my son there were three main reasons that kept me writing this book until I finished it. The first reason why I started writing and kept writing was because I wanted to give my son a book that he could take with him off to college so that even though I wasn't around that my voice and my guidance regarding manhood would be at his fingertips whenever he wanted it or needed it. Secondly, I kept writing this book because I was convinced that the information in this book would be a helpful guide to aid other young males that may not have a father figure around to give them advice about becoming a man. Lastly I wrote this book as part of the legacy that I wanted to leave behind after my time on this earth has expired. Writing this book would ensure that my words, my thoughts and my advice would live on long after I'm gone and there would be something tangible that I left behind for others to benefit from.

Leaving a legacy is the expected dues that every man that has had the privilege of walking this earth is required to pay. Leaving your legacy is not only your way of letting the world know that you were here but your legacy is the gift that you leave behind that will keep on giving long after you're gone. History and every day conversation is full of stories of men whose legacies are deeply cemented in our everyday culture. Carnegie, Ford, JP Morgan, Rockefeller, Kennedy, Martin Luther King Jr, Toussaint L'Ouverture are just a few men that have long past but their legacy continues to live and make an impact on the lives of millions of people that were not even born when these men were around. Legacy building should always be a motivating factor in just about everything that you do. You should always ask yourself, is what I'm doing aligned with my mission in life as a man and the legacy that I want to leave behind. There are several ways that a man can leave a legacy and it is your choice what legacy you choose to leave behind. In one of my favorite books, Proverbs 13:22 states: A good man leaveth an inheritance to his children's children. This verse speaks directly to leaving a legacy not only for your children but your grandchildren as well. Leaving a legacy or inheritance is not a suggestion to a man but a solemn oath that he must make within himself if he wishes to complete his mission as a man.

My father grew up in the rural south on a farm where he was one several children. By most standards it was safe to assume that my grandparents were not rich. They lived in a little old house near the end of a long dusty one lane country road. I remember going to their house as a kid and we would ask my grandfather what was that little building in the back of the house and he explained to us that it was an outhouse.

My father later stated that they had just gotten indoor plumbing and running water in the house a few years after I was born which would have been in the 1970's. It's hard to believe now that running water in a house was a luxury at one point and still is for some places within the United States. My grandparent's house was small by any standards but it was extremely small considering the amount of children that were raised there. We would run through what seemed like miles of open fields where you could find horses, cows and eat peaches from the peach farms just up the dusty road from my grandparent's house. As a young teenager my grandfather passed away and he was buried in the family cemetery just across the field from my grandparent's home. Several years after that, my grandmother passed away and she too was also buried in the family cemetery.

After my grandparents passed away my father would sometimes talk about the responsibility of handling the affairs of their estate. I thought to myself that the word estate was a fancy word for such a simple house and an outbuilding. I would then learn that the house that my grandparents live in and owned was situated on several acres of land that stretched as far as my eyes could see and that the family owned all of it. The fields that we ran in, the horses, the cows, the ditches and gullies and yes even the outhouse were all owned by my grandparents and their children. With a very limited education, which was not uncommon back in my grandparent's days, they were able to leave a legacy to not only their children but to their children's children's children and beyond. My grandparents left an inheritance that was far beyond my ability to really appreciate until recently when I started thinking about what legacy could I and would I leave behind for my children's children.

A few years ago I was at the "family estate" as I affectionately called it and I sat on the porch of a home that my father had built for my grandmother while she was alive. I sat on the porch and I watched my children and my nephew run around the yard just like we did when we were their age and as I looked at them I was thinking that they didn't even know the legacy that they were standing on.

I made it a point to gather my children and we walked the property and the street that grandparents live on. As my father and some of my uncles and cousins were walking along with us I purposely asked my father and uncles questions about how my grandparents obtained the property that we were enjoying. As my father, my children and I made our way across the field to the family cemetery I couldn't help but feel the presence of a comforting spirit with every step we took toward the sacred grounds of my grandparent's final resting place.

As we walked through the family cemetery and stood at my grandparent's grave I couldn't help but feel a sense of pride because I felt connected to the legacy that they left behind. The legacy wasn't the land or property that had me beaming with pride. The legacy was the stories that I got to hear that I never heard of and the fact that my children would know some of where they came from. My pride was in the fact that I was standing in a place where I could see a minimum of 5 generations of people all standing in one spot. All of us loved each other, got along and were all standing on and in our legacy at the same time. As I stood there reading the tombstones in our family cemetery I glanced up and paused for a few seconds and stood there in silence. I looked at my son and my daughter and I looked around as far as I could see and it dawned on me that this is what Proverbs 13:22 looked like. I always wondered if my grandparents had their grandchildren and great-great grandchildren in mind when they started their legacy many years ago. I often wondered what legacy and inheritance I would leave my children and grandchildren and what legacy I would leave my family in general. I also wondered what legacy I would leave my community, my church and charitable organizations. Leaving a legacy is one of our missions as a man and its one mission that we can't afford not to accomplish. A huge part of what will be considered your level of success will be measured in how successful you were in leaving a legacy behind that future generations will be able to benefit from and enjoy. You can look around just about anywhere and see the legacies that men have left. The Ford automobile, The Ford foundation, Carnegie libraries and foundations, The Duke endowment, The

Gates foundation all carry the names of the men who made sure that they would leave a lasting legacy to help others and to make the world a better place. What legacy will you leave as a man? What will be your gift to society? Leaving a legacy should be at the forefront of everything that you do as a man for it will be the footprint that you leave behind to let the world know that you were here long after you are gone. Your legacy may be your offspring that carry your name, a scholarship fund, a building named in your honor or the positive impressions that you leave on the people that you meet. Each one of us has something to leave for the next generation and the sooner we start to work on the legacy that we wish to leave the more purpose our lives will have.

The Dash by Linda Ellis

I read of a man who stood to speak at the funeral of a friend. He referred to the dates on her casket from beginning to the end.

He noted that first came the date of her birth and spoke of the following date with tears, but he said what mattered most of all was the dash between those years.

For that dash represents all the time that she spent alive on earth and now only those who loved her know what that little line is worth. For it matters not, how much we own, the cars, the house, the cash, What matters is how we live and love and how we spend our dash.

So think about this long and hard; are there things you would like to change? For you never know how much time is left that can still be rearranged.

If we could just slow down enough to consider what is true and real and always try to understand the way other people feel.

And be less quick to anger and show appreciation more and love the people in our lives like we have never loved before.

If we treat each other with respect and more often wear a smile, remembering that this special dash might only last a little while.

So when your eulogy is being read with your life's actions to rehash would you be proud of the things they say about how you spent your dash?

Legacy Quotes

"We don't inherit the earth from our ancestors, we borrow it from our children." — David Brower

"Our days are numbered. One of the primary goals in our lives should be to prepare for our last day. The legacy we leave is not just in our possessions, but in the quality of our lives. What preparations should we be making now? The greatest waste in all of our earth, which cannot be recycled or reclaimed, is our waste of the time that God has given us each day." — Bill Graham

"Language allows us to reach out to people, to touch them with our innermost fears, hopes, disappointments, victories. To reach out to people we'll never meet. It's the greatest legacy you could ever leave your children or your loved ones: The history of how you felt."— Simon Van Booy

"Build the legacy that aligns with God and do it right in satan's face." — Dexsta Ray

Legacies That A Man Should Consider Leaving

Continuously Pray That God Gives Your Children A Sense Of Purpose, Direction And Mission- *Teach and leave your children a strong heritage of who they are and where they came from. This can be accomplished by taking them to family reunions and encouraging them to spend time with their grandparents and the more aged members of their family where they can dialogue and gain knowledge about their family history. Live a life that your children can be proud of and would like to imitate without losing who they are as individuals. Leave them with a good name and protect it at all cost. Teach your children and those around you about having a purpose and a mission. I once heard someone say that "Our children are messengers that we send to a time that we ourselves will never see."*

Become A Mentor Or Start A Mentor Organization- *It is every man's duty to prepare the next generation of young men to be able to carry on the legacy that we leave behind and to do greater than what we were able to do. A strong mentor program will continue to give long after you're gone.*

Leave The Places You Go And The People You Meet Better Than You Found Them- A legacy does not only come from creating and leaving something physical and literal. A legacy can come from an idea, a tradition, a thought, anything that changes a person or the world and leaves them both better than you found them.

Financial Gifts That Takes Care Of God's People- One of the most impactful gifts that you can give is a financial legacy gift designed to take care of the needs of people. You can leave a financial legacy gift in the form of scholarship, a foundation, life insurance policies, planned giving or a named will.

The Gift Of Faith And Hope- *There is going to come a time when all a person has is faith and hope. These two gifts will carry you through the best of times and they will carry you through the worst of times. It is one of the greatest gifts that you can share with a person. It is the gift that can last a lifetime and can be passed on from generation to generation.*

Write A Book- *Leaving your stories, your experiences, your thoughts and your wisdom in the form of a book is a gift that will live long after you're gone. Your words and your thoughts get an opportunity to live forever in a book.*

Give Of Yourself-*There is only one you on the entire face of the earth. Each time a person has the opportunity to be in your presence it should be a present, a gift. Give them you and everything that makes you unique. The world will never be able to experience you again after you're gone. Live knowing that you take nothing with you, empty yourself and leave it here.*

Motivational Videos On Fatherhood
Please watch as least two videos below on Fatherhood

Fatherhood- How to earn honor Myles Munroe
YouTube

President Obama Speaks About Fatherhood   YouTube

Fatherhood Advice For Dads- TD Jakes
YouTube

The Power Of A Father- Dr. Charles Stanley
YouTube

5 Things That Make A Great Father- TD Jakes
YouTube

Conclusion

Thank you for reading this book and I hope that you found it to be insightful, informative and practical. This book was designed to evoke dialogue with your sons and other young males and to give them a man's perspective on some of the areas of life that they will be encountering. Some of you may already be at that coveted destination of being a Man and a Father and you are enjoying the fruits of your labor. If that is the case, then I hope that you found something within these pages that will aid in taking and maintaining you to your next level. We all are still a work in progress and with just a few minor adjustments in our mindsets and behaviors we will gradually find ourselves becoming the Men and Fathers that we really want to be.

Each chapter discussed in this book I discussed with my son in detail and it was some very interesting conversations. I learned a lot from having an open and honest dialogue with my son about the things that I know he would need to know about. The more I discussed the topics in this book the more I realized that there is still a lot that I need to work on myself. The road to Fatherhood and Manhood is not a destination it is a journey as you will never get everything right or become the perfect human being. Writing this book opened my eyes to the fact that while I have accomplished some things that I could be proud of there is still so much more that I could and should be doing as a Father and as a Man. If you have anything that you would like to discuss that you read in this book feel free to contact me as my email address can be found in the about the author section at the end of this book. I look forward to hearing from you and feel free to leave your reviews or comments. Once you have finished reading this book please share it with another young father, man, single mother or anyone that is raising a male that you feel can benefit from its contents. Peace and Blessings

Songs That I listened To As I Wrote This Book

My testimony- Marvin Sapp

 Praise him in advance- Marvin Sapp

 He has his hands on Me-Marvin Sapp

Praise you forever- Marvin Sapp

Here I am- Marvin Sapp

What shall I do- James Cleveland

IOU Me- BeBe & CeCe Winans

After the Dance- Marvin Gaye

Heaven must be like this- Ohio Players

Lady- The Whispers

Knocks me off my feet - Stevie Wonder

Aja - Steely Dan

Bashir Hogue- My Praise, My Worship's for Real

Angel-Anita Baker

Does anybody really know what time it is- Chicago

Don't worry bout a thing- Stevie Wonder

Wake up everybody- Teddy Pendergrass and the blue notes

Ice box-Omarion,

If you think you're lonely now- Bobby Womack

If you leave me now- Chicago

Insatiable- Prince

If I was your girlfriend- Prince

Anniversary- Tony Toni Tone'

Jingling baby- LL Cool J

Here comes the lords- lords of the underground

Make me a believer -Luther Vandross

Other Side of the world- Luther Vandross

Human nature- Miles Davis

Give me the reason– Luther Vandross

Love under new management- Mikki Howard

My life- Mary J bilge

U send me swinging- Mint Condition

Can You Stand the rain- New Edition

Never felt this way- Brian Mcknight

I'd die without you–Pm Dawn

Rain – SWV

Weak- SWV

Someone to love- Mint Condition

For You- Kenny Lattimore

Strange and Beautiful- Aqualung

Summer Breeze- Isley Brothers

Sensuality 1&2- Isley brothers

Highway of my life- Isley Brothers

Get me bodied- Beyonce

Bashir Hogue-Random

Stomp-Brothers Johnson

Side Show- Blue Magic

What's come over me- Blue Magic

Practice what you preach- Barry White

There it is- Barry White

Spend my life with you-Tamia

Tomorrow- Winans

Tomorrow a better you- Tevin Campbell

Ain't no need to worry- The Winans & Anita Baker

Tokyo Blue- Najee

About The Author

Bestselling author **Calvin E. Clark Sr.** received his Bachelor's of Science degree in Accounting from Livingstone College and has worked in corporate America for the past 20 years with industry experience in payroll management, commercial underwriting, pension administration and internal auditing. Mr. Clark has been recognized as a corporate change leader and most recently was part of a team of change leaders that were nominated as finalist for "The Most Innovative Approach To Driving Cultural Change" at the 2015 Global PEX awards held in Orlando, Florida. Mr. Clark wrote and published his first bestselling book titled: **10 Laws of Manhood** that has been used in men's conferences and workshops throughout the country. Mr. Clark is a servant leader with a humble heart that is actively involved in his community and his church. Mr. Clark received the **2015 Gospel Image Award for Best New Inspirational Author** for the Book **Strong Fathers, Strong Sons, Strong Men**. Mr. Clark is the proud father of a teenage son and a teenage daughter that are a constant reminder of why it is important that he stays true to his mission as a Man and as a Father. Mr. Clark enjoys boating, riding motorcycles, photography and spending time with his family. To contact Mr. Clark he can be reached at: 10lawsofmanhood@gmail.com .

Journal Notes On Things You Can Do To Become A Better Father And A Better Man

30 Day Goal Setting Journal

30 Day Goal Setting Journal

30 Day Goal Setting Journal

30 Day Goal Setting Journal

30 Day Goal Setting Journal

30 Day Goal Setting Journal

30 Day Goal Setting Journal

30 Day Goal Setting Journal

30 Day Goal Setting Journal

30 Day Goal Setting Journal

30 Day Goal Setting Journal

30 Day Goal Setting Journal

30 Day Goal Setting Journal

30 Day Goal Setting Journal

30 Day Goal Setting Journal

30 Day Goal Setting Journal

30 Day Goal Setting Journal

30 Day Goal Setting Journal

30 Day Goal Setting Journal

30 Day Goal Setting Journal

30 Day Goal Setting Journal

30 Day Goal Setting Journal

30 Day Goal Setting Journal

30 Day Goal Setting Journal

30 Day Goal Setting Journal

30 Day Goal Setting Journal

30 Day Goal Setting Journal

30 Day Goal Setting Journal

30 Day Goal Setting Journal

30 Day Goal Setting Journal

30 Day Goal Setting Journal

30 Day Goal Setting Journal

30 Day Goal Setting Journal

30 Day Goal Setting Journal

30 Day Goal Setting Journal

30 Day Goal Setting Journal

30 Day Goal Setting Journal

30 Day Goal Setting Journal

30 Day Goal Setting Journal

30 Day Goal Setting Journal

30 Day Goal Setting Journal

30 Day Goal Setting Journal

30 Day Goal Setting Journal

30 Day Goal Setting Journal

30 Day Goal Setting Journal

30 Day Goal Setting Journal

30 Day Goal Setting Journal

30 Day Goal Setting Journal

30 Day Goal Setting Journal

30 Day Goal Setting Journal

30 Day Goal Setting Journal

30 Day Goal Setting Journal

30 Day Goal Setting Journal

30 Day Goal Setting Journal

Day Goal Setting Journal

30 Day Goal Setting Journal

30 Day Goal Setting Journal

30 Day Goal Setting Journal

30 Day Goal Setting Journal

30 Day Goal Setting Journal

30 Day Goal Setting Journal

30 Day Goal Setting Journal

30 Day Goal Setting Journal

30 Day Goal Setting Journal

30 Day Goal Setting Journal

30 Day Goal Setting Journal

30 Day Goal Setting Journal

30 Day Goal Setting Journal

30 Day Goal Setting Journal

30 Day Goal Setting Journal

30 Day Goal Setting Journal

30 Day Goal Setting Journal

30 Day Goal Setting Journal

30 Day Goal Setting Journal

30 Day Goal Setting Journal

30 Day Goal Setting Journal

30 Day Goal Setting Journal

30 Day Goal Setting Journal

\

30 Day Goal Setting Journal

30 Day Goal Setting Journal

30 Day Goal Setting Journal

30 Day Goal Setting Journal

30 Day Goal Setting Journal

30 Day Goal Setting Journal

30 Day Goal Setting Journal

30 Day Goal Setting Journal

30 Day Goal Setting Journal

30 Day Goal Setting Journal

30 Day Goal Setting Journal

30 Day Goal Setting Journal

30 Day Goal Setting Journal

30 Day Goal Setting Journal

30 Day Goal Setting Journal

30 Day Goal Setting Journal

30 Day Goal Setting Journal

30 Day Goal Setting Journal

30 Day Goal Setting Journal

30 Day Goal Setting Journal

30 Day Goal Setting Journal

30 Day Goal Setting Journal

30 Day Goal Setting Journal

30 Day Goal Setting Journal

30 Day Goal Setting Journal

30 Day Goal Setting Journal

30 Day Goal Setting Journal

30 Day Goal Setting Journal

30 Day Goal Setting Journal

30 Day Goal Setting Journal

30 Day Goal Setting Journal

30 Day Goal Setting Journal

30 Day Goal Setting Journal

30 Day Goal Setting Journal

30 Day Goal Setting Journal

30 Day Goal Setting Journal

30 Day Goal Setting Journal

30 Day Goal Setting Journal

30 Day Goal Setting Journal

30 Day Goal Setting Journal

30 Day Goal Setting Journal

30 Day Goal Setting Journal

30 Day Goal Setting Journal

30 Day Goal Setting Journal

30 Day Goal Setting Journal

30 Day Goal Setting Journal

30 Day Goal Setting Journal

30 Day Goal Setting Journal

Made in the USA
Columbia, SC
29 August 2022

66233744R00159